European Identity: The Newly Born European Demos?

Endri Shqerra

Table of Contents

Introduction

In a solemn address to the opening ceremony of the "International Peace Conference" held in Paris in August 1849, Viktor Hugo prophesized the dawn of a European Union in this spirit:

> "...A day shall come when you will no longer make wars..... And in that day you will all have one common thought, common interest, a common destiny; you will embrace each other and recognize each other as children of the same blood, and of the same race; that day you will no longer be hostile tribes, - you will be a people... A day will come when you...[will]...be blended into a superior unity, and constitute an European fraternity, just as Normandy, Burgundy, Lorraine, Alsace, have been blended into France.... A day will come when bullets and bomb-shells will be replaced by votes, by the universal suffrage of nations, by the venerable arbitration of a great Sovereign Senate, which will be to Europe what the Parliament is to England, what the Diet is to Germany, what the Legislative Assembly is to France. ....A day will come when these two immense groups, the United States of America and the United States of Europe shall be seen placed in presence of each other..." [Hugo, 1849, 11].

Justifiably classified amongst the visionary fathers of EU, Hugo firmly believed that it would not be "necessary that four hundred years should pass away for that day to come" [Hugo 1849, 12]. Today, much less than four hundred years from Hugo's statement, Europe has reached this day in the form of the European Union. On the way, the European Union was successful in crafting a common identity of the peoples of its member states primarily based on common beliefs and by way of votes, and neither bullets nor bomb-shells, in establishing a Parliament. In full vindication of Victor Hugo's vision, the EU and the U.S.A. are now two leading world powers.

Through single market, political unity, and common history post-national theory argues, European funds and activities aiming at promoting cultural exchanges are further targeting at the construction of a common European cultural community.

Even at the time of the Maastricht Treaty (1993), itself viewed as the treaty which "established the European Union (EU)" [Maastricht Treaty. 2012], and, by inference, the political unity of Europe, Bakke [1993, 2] recognized that the quintessence of European solidarity (European identity) relies on what comes beyond a political and economic union: "A sense of European solidarity becomes even more vital if the integration is to proceed past the political and economic union envisaged in the Maastricht treaty." The establishment of a European Constitution, which in itself would represent the federal stage of Europe, shall result in a stronger European solidarity and in a more consolidated European identity. This view, as I shall demonstrate, is also advocated by the 'constitutional patriotism' theory.

In addition to the establishment of the constitution, the further evolution of European identity is also related with the erosion of national identities. Interesting is the fact that, as Herman [2004, 41] argues "Modern nationalism was born in Europe, and it is there where some scholars and politicians are mounting a death watch" of nationalism. The decline of nationalism as a general statement is somehow accepted by other scholars like Delanty, Sindic and Smith but, the controversy between them, as we will demonstrate in chapter 3, lies to what degree will the decline of nationalism in Europe leads to the replacement of national identities by European identity. Delanty [2005, 2] maintains that European identity will stand above national identities of Europe as British identity stands beyond Irish, Wales, Scottish and English identities. Smith [1991, 170], on the other hand, maintains that European identity will not even resemble the British models. In spite of their different views, their common conclusion is that European identity will not replace or supersede national identities in the foreseeable future. Quoting Delanty and

Smith, Rambour [2005, 3] argues that Delanty does not conceive Europe as a political community because he conceives national identities as strong. He [2005, 3] further calls Smith too as a strong supporter of nationalism who argues that European identity is not able to elicit the loyalty and mobilization that nationalism is able to do.

Similar to the Delanty's [2005, 2] concept of the pyramid of identities, One's [2004, 34] approach this matter not as a competition but rather as a co-existence of European and national identities in the form of multiple identities: "there is not necessarily a *zero-sum struggle* between a national and a European identity. People have always had *multiple identities*". Because of the increasing globalization and cosmopolitanism people nowadays are having dual and even multiple identities, which enable the co-existence of national and European identity [Delanty 1996, 2].

In 2005, EU failed in the ratification of its important document - the constitution. The failure of the Constitutional Treaty (2005) seemed to convey the idea that the process of the European integration had reached its highest limits and could not go much further as to establish its constitution. Hence, a stronger European identity which represents the sense of community and the sense of belonging was necessary in order to inspire people to follow their elites and even to affect EU policies through public spheres. The failure of the European Constitutional Treaty and the subsequent stagnation of deeper EU integration were conditioned, as we shall demonstrate in chapter 2, by the low degree of consolidation of the European identity.

Four years before the Constitutional Treaty (2005), Habermas [2001, 15] wondered whether Europe was ready to establish a constitution, representing a higher integrated Europe and the federal stage of EU. Eurosceptics claimed that there is no European *demos* and as such EU should not have a constitution.

7

Their skeptic position was evident in their No Demos thesis, a decision held by the German Federal Constitutional Court. Habermas [2001, 15] criticizes their conceptualization of *demos* based on national theories and argues about the existence of a European civic *demos.*

The main question this book tries to answer is whether European identity will replace or supersede national identities of Europe; a question related with the nature of European and national identities, with possible evolution of European identity (assisted by the establishment of the constitution) as well as with the erosion of national identities in Europe. The principal argument there is that: different from national identities, the European identity develops in the fashion analyzed by post-national theory, through civic rights, "constitutional patriotism", and through its developing common culture. It is the post-national nature of European identity which enables it to develop alongside national identities, even if national identities are strong and cannot be replaced by European identity.

The evolution of European identity is related with the establishment of the constitution. In this thesis I shall demonstrate the mutual relationship between European identity and the constitution. As it shall be argued, the existences of a Constitution, or similar institutions in the form of treaties, further the degree of consolidation of a European identity and of European integration. This view is hold and by 'constitutional patriotism' theory. Said differently, it is the consolidation degree of European identity which affects the success of constitutional ratification and, vice-versa, the failure of the constitution implies a low degree of consolidation of European identity.

Chapter 1 delves into matters centered around the definition of "identity", its derivatives (identification, multiple identities, identity shifts, national and post-national identity, constitutional patriotism) and their relations. Approaching these terms from a ...ety of theoretical perspectives (primordial, constructivist, post-...tional, cosmopolitanism and globalization), the chapter, utilizing secondary and primary evidence extrapolated from Pan-European surveys, ultimately constructs a definition of the European identity: a western European continental sense of belonging to a European community comprising primarily post-national, but also national, elements, not least based on Europe's perceived common history.

Chapter 2 deals with the failure of Constitutional Treaty. The failure of the European Constitutional Treaty's ratification in France and the Netherlands was primarily owed to the predominance of domestic politics over the matter at vote resulting in an identity shift of loyalty from EU to the national state. This failure, however, enhanced European public spheres, thereby enforcing the collective identity of the European political community. The further consolidation of the European identity shall contribute to the success of the constitutional ratification in the EU, since, as the Swiss paradigm demonstrates, both of these need to develop simultaneously.

Chapter 3 deals with the erosion of national identities in Europe and their strengths. The question dealt in this chapter is whether European identity will be able to replace or supersede national identities of Europe. The main finding of this chapter is that national identities have not declined. They continue to comprise 91% of Europeans. On the other hand, as I shall demonstrate in chapter 3, more people are identifying themselves as Europeans, which means a multiple identity for Europeans. This suggests that national identities have lost their role as the only or the dominant mean of identification.

The post-national character of the European identity alongside cosmopolitanism and globalization are gradually eroding national identities of EU member states. Notwithstanding, national identities in the EU are still strong, as the European identity shall not supersede them, since their compatibility enables their *symbiosis* and parallel development.

Subsequently, there exists a civic European *demos* in political/legal terms, which, alike the European identity, is complementary to the national *demos* of EU member states. Alongside these points presented in chapter 4, we shall continue and with some scholarly criticisms about the 'No Demos Thesis' and the ethno/cultural approach.

The method that I will widely use mostly is the case study method coupled with analysis. In chapter 2 I will use the analogical reasoning by comparing the EU case with the establishment of the constitution in Switzerland. In my research, I will use top-bottom approach as well as the bottom-up approaches, with the later as the principal approach. Top-bottom approach of studying the European identity is to analyze the degree of consolidation of the European identity induced by policies of EU. The bottom-up approach of studying European identity is by studying individuals, the way and the degree they feel Europeans.

Identity and European Identity: Historical and Theoretical Perspectives

Individual identity is a psychological identity whereas national identity or the identity based on a larger community is a social identity. There are the forms of association of the individual with larger communities which co-determine the individual national identity [Jackobs, D. and Maier, R, 1998, 3]. Balibar, E. and Wallerstain, I, [1991, 94] too, assert that "all identity is individual, but there is no individual identity that is not...constructed within a field of social values, norms of behavior and collective symbols. The real question is how the dominant reference points of individual identity change over time and with the changing institutional environment" (my emphasis). In this last sentence, Balibar and Wallerstain clearly hint identity shifts, which, as we shall demonstrate in chapters 2-4, is the case of Europeans because of "the changing institutional environment" [1991. 94] in Europe.

An important aspect of identification is its mechanism of exclusion, as it always results in the formation of a "we", i.e. the members of the community and the "others" or 'foreigners' who are excluded from this community [Rousseau and Veen [2005, 689]. Social identity draws compelling lines for its members; members of the community regard themselves as the same with others inside the line and different from the members of other communities. The feeling of belonging is associated with feeling of exclusion for those who do not belong in the community [Herman 2004, 48]. To reveal the nature of the identity in this chapter we shall study the definition of identity through a variety of theoretical perspectives, the concept of the European identity as well as its history.

Premordialism ascribes certain rigidity to identity and emphasizes the emotional power of the identification's constituents. Rousseau and Veen [2005, 688] criticize premordialists who claim that "identity becomes fixed once it is acquired." Thus, primordialists reject the notion of identity shift advocated by Rousseau and Veen [688] as well as by the constructivist theory, as we shall present below. Primordialists also view identification as an emotional response of the individual in rapport with its environment; "True identity depends on the support which the young individual receives from the collective sense of identity characterizing the social groups significant to him: his class, his nation, his culture." [Edwards, 2009, p. 20] (my emphasis). Tajfel [1981, 55] also emphasizes the emotional charge of national identification by describing identity as: "that part of an individual's self-concept which derives from his knowledge of his membership of a social group (or groups) together with the value and emotional significance attached to that membership". Smith [1991, 175] was apparently familiar with such theories when he acknowledged the "emotional mobilization that nationalism is able to erect", the strongest property of nationalism and national identities, after him.

Constructivists argue that nations are comprised of "imagined communities", hence, a national identity is not something that people inherently possess but rather something which can be constructed or engineered [Anderson 1991, 6-7]. Their view is that identities are not static but can change, depending on different factors. They argue that people have multiple identities and social factors can cause a shift in identities [Rousseau, D. and Veen, M. 2005, 688]. Rousseau and Veen [2005, 688] further emphasizes the role of situational context in the identity shifts: "Individuals possess multiple identities and often shift from one identity to another….the context of the situation can alter which identity moves into the foreground".

Constructivists further argue that the selection of identities depend on political and economic structures. Having multiples identities enable people to adopt the identity they want in accordance with economic incentives such as the access to jobs, markets and lands. The shift of identity in this case is a preference based on interest and on reasonable calculations. Through this, political institutions can encourage the adaptation as well as the emergence of some identities and in the same time they can discourage and erode other identities [Rousseau, D. and Veen, M. 2005, 689].

Though national identities, viewed by a constructivists or primordialists angle, seem strong and powerful "it is important to appreciate that national identity is far more likely to be a contested idea today than one that can be worn lightly" [Delanty, G, 1996, 8]. Globalization, as we shall demonstrate in chapter 3, erodes national identities through technology which facilitates the communication between cultures. The political unity, as demonstrated by the case of Switzerland that we shall demonstrate in chapter 2, is able to produce a collective identity of its community even in the absence of a common language and culture, i.e. two indispensable constituents of the premordialist notion of national identity.

Globalization and Cosmopolitanism, as we shall also demonstrate in chapter 3, erode national identities and nationalism and result in the creation of a global culture and cosmopolitan identity. Thus, a new identity emerges which differs from national identities. This cosmopolitan identity created by cosmopolitan factors is very important in maintaining peace in the world. It creates a shared identity for all nations. As a result, the formation of "we" the citizens of the world reduces the likelihood of war and increases the international cooperation [Rousseau and Veen 2005, 686] Shared identity possessed by democratic countries may even be the third causal mechanism, after similar norms and structures, in the "democratic peace theory" [2005, 688]. It is the shared identity that democratic countries possess which reduces the likelihood of war between them.

Different from national identities and even stronger than the global identity created by globalization and cosmopolitanism, "post-national identity is..... a political identity founded on the recognition

13

of democratic norms and human rights, as these are embedded in a particular constitutional tradition" [Eriksen 2009, 38]. Hobson [2003, 139] argues that unlike national identities which are based on ethnical orientation and on the common culture, post-national identity "is founded on the constitutional principles anchored in the political culture and not on the basic ethical orientations of the cultural form of life predominant in that country".

Eurobarometer 71 [2009, 39] indicates the most important elements which Europeans think to make up the European identity [Table 1]. In 2009, 41% of Europeans selected 'democratic values' as one of the two most important elements that make up European identity. 24% define civic rights or social protections, 11% list entrepreneurship, 25% define geographic position as an important element of European identity, 24% define common history as an important element, 8% list the common religious heritage, 5% claim that there is no European identity, 23% define the common culture [Eurobarometer 71, 39]. Democratic values (41%) and civic rights (24%) are essential part in the post-national theory. Geographic position (25%) in this case does not indicate territoriality in the way that nationalism does. The common religion (8%) is a component of nationalism since the religious groups usually represents larger communities than the nation. The common culture (23%) belongs to both national and post-national theories. Common history (24%) is part of national theories. Figures indicate that European identity, above all, is a post-national identity (65%) which also comprises national elements. We may define it as a Western European continental sense of belonging to a European community comprising primarily post-national, but also national, elements, not least based on Europe's perceived common history, constructing a pyramid of identities with the *sui generis* European identity at its top.

Table 1

Most important elements that Europeans think to make up European
identity.

Democratic values	41%
Geographic position	25%
Civic rights or social protections	24%
Common history	24%
Common culture	23%
Entrepreneurship	11%
Common religious heritage	8%
There is no European identity	5%

Source: Eurobarometer 71 [39]

Globalization is one of the most important theories which
helps in the evolution of European identity by eroding national
identities. There are the improvements in the information
technology, in communication and transport which give people more
possibilities to pass the boundaries of their nation, to get in touch
with people of other nations and to learn about other cultures. This
interaction results in the diminishing role of national identities and
cultures and gives people more choices to develop and maintain the

identities they want and to shift in identities without considering nationalism [Sindic 2008, 7]. It is, therefore, evident that globalization stresses the role of communication between different cultures through the information technology, which results in the diminishing role of nationalism as well as in the creation of a global culture [2008, 7]. Thanks to technology, people get information and communicate with people from all over the world, thereby making intercultural communication possible. The amount of information easily accessed by the internet has made national boundaries less and less relevant *"turning the planet into a 'global village…'"* [Sindic, D. 2008, 7]. People can nowadays easily travel in different countries and even stay there. They learn about other countries' cultures. Their friendship and acquaintance is also stretch beyond their national boundaries. As a result of these shared experiences "cultural differences between nations are becoming more and more blurred while cultural hegemony within the nation is becoming more fragmented…..(and) everyday life is less and less framed by nationalist practices….thus the feeling of shared experiences and information with others is no longer concurrent with the limits of nation" [2008, 5]. Furthermore, supra-national entities like the EU and other global economic and political organizations limit the sovereignty states, reduce the role of nationalism, and assist in creating a global culture [2008, 8].

Cosmopolitanism, another theory supporting the further evolution of European identity, derives from a Greek word *kosmopolites* which literally means 'citizen of the world'. It suggests that we belong to the whole world not to a part of it. It presupposes that we are citizens of the world and emphasizes the idea of a "world state" where people are all equal. It means to be free from national ideas and prejudices. "Cosmopolitanism considers the case of a world society governed according to the principles of human rights and justice" [Rambour, 2005].

Cosmopolitanism, which Delanty [2009, 35] considers as "one of the most important ways of making sense of the present world", originates in ancient times. The birth of Cosmopolitanism has been influenced by Alexander the Great's (356-323 B.C.) efforts to create an 'world empire'. It gained impetus during the Roman Empire and later on in the Enlightenment whose thinkers and writers used cosmopolitan elements and ideas in their works [Leoussi and Smith 2001, 35]. Reilly, K. [2004, 209] wrote: "at the core of Enlightenment was the idea that people could use reason to overcome the bias and self-interest of their own region, nation, religion, group, or tribe and emphasize with a larger group", citing Voltaire's *Treatise on Toleration* (1763). [cited in Reilly 2004, 211]: "I say we should regard all men as our brothers. What? The Turk my brother?...Yes, without doubt; are we not all children of the same father and creatures of the same God". Though such ideas were cast by a Frenchman in France and primarily for his fellow Frenchmen, they also shattered in France. The universal "rights of man", rights hold as human beings as well as citizens of the world, were restricted only to the members of the nation. The principles of the enlightenment were eventually corrupted by the French Revolution, nationalism and chauvinism [Leoussi, A. Smith, A. 2001, 35].

Nowadays cosmopolitanism has regained impetus in the construction and studies of the European identity. Delanty [2005, 4] attaches some cosmopolitan meaning to the European identity when he asserts that "to be European is simply to recognize that one lives in a world that does not belong to a specific people". With the decline of nationalism, the cosmopolitan identity has become increasingly topical. According to the study of Euroakademia [2012] "Europe cores the highest in the level of cosmopolitan identity... That is why it is so important to consider cosmopolitanism in the study of European supranational identities". Eurobarometer 71 [2009, 34] indicates that in 2008, 59% of Europeans felt as citizens of the world whereas in 2009 the cosmopolitan identity in Europe increased to a record rate of 64%.

Post-national theory, the basic theory of European identity, presupposes the death of the national era and the emergence of a new era without nations. It suggests that the single market, the political unity, and the common culture and history influence the emergence of the post-national era. Proponents of this theory suggest that a new kind of identity can emerge which will stand beyond traditions of a particular nation [Rambour, M. 2005 p. 5]. Political community and solidarity of the people is not seen as created through common ethnicity and language but through civic rights that citizens hold. These rights make all citizens equal by stressing the political community without regarding them as minority groups, as nation-states do. Eriksen [2009, 38] argues that "Citizens should be seen as bound to each other not by those pre-political ties that nation-states have applied to but by subscription to democratic procedures and human rights".

'Constitutional patriotism' was first projected by Sternberger in 1990 as a theory for European identity [Stojanovic 2003, 79]. After him, Habermas redeveloped this theory. The impact of this theory in the European integration has been huge because it argues for the creation of a *demos* detached from ethnic ties, as it is the case of EU. Breda [2011, 1] writes that "since its first appearance just over a decade ago, Habermas' constitutional patriotism has inspired a rich and articulate series of theoretical analyses and has indirectly encouraged constitutional projects such as the Constitution for Europe".

'Constitutional patriotism', the source of inspiration for European identity, is a type of post-national theory. In "constitutional patriotism", people are loyal to the constitution and to the democratic values. They are united by the constitution rather than by the common culture or ethnic tradition [Delantly 1996, 9]. Thomas, D. Schult, Ch. Zuber, H. [2011] define 'constitutional patriotism' as: "the patriotism of global citizens who are concerned about human rights,....where citizens feel a sense of patriotism based on their shared political values rather than a shared ethnic identity or language".

Having outlined above the principal theories on identities and identification processes, I shall now focus on how these theories can be utilized in our understanding of the European identity. The constructivist theory of identity formation explains the present situation of identity shift in Europe from national to the European identity. As Rousseau, D. and Veen, M. [2005, 689] argue, it is the EU itself which influences in the adaption of its collective identity through political and economic integration. The source of loyalty for European identity is 'constitutional patriotism'. Its solidarity is founded on civic rights, rather than common origin and history.

European identity, with its roots in ancient Roman Empire, gained new impetus in Maastricht Treaty which first established the 'European Community'. "Throughout the Treaty: (1) The term 'European Economic Community' shall be replaced by the term 'European Community'" [The Maastricht Treaty 1992, 2]. The establishment of the 'European Community' brought into foreground the need for a strong European identity as a collective identity of the European political community. This need required and an academic study of European identity. Many authors began to publish their works about European identity like: Schlesinger in 1992, Smith in 1992, Habermas in 1992 and Delanty in 1995 [Walkenhorst,H. 2009, 6]. The Laeken Declaration of 2000 on the future of the European Union emphasized the urgent need for the consolidation of the European identity which served as a political identity [CVCE 2001]. Another effort in consolidating European identity, similar with how nation-states engineered their identities, is the emphasize on Roman Empire as the common history of Europeans as well as the origin of European identity itself.

Scholarly views on European identity differ. "While some scholars believe that European identity is a form of cosmopolitanism (hence a post-national identity), others consider it as a form of nationalism on a new level" [Euroakademia, 2012]. Among scholars who consider European identity as a post-national identity we can mention; Habermas, Rambour, Jackob, Valentini, Walkenhorst, Guler, etc. Among scholars who consider European identity as a new form of national identity we can mention: Smith, Delanty, Sindic, Kaelberer, Clinpoes, Oner etc.

Perhaps the most beautiful, though not post-national, definition of European identity is that of Delanty's. Delanty [2005, 2], at the time when the Constitutional Treaty failed, described the European identity as a "pyramid of identities" composed of different national identities with the European identity on the top, just as British identity stands above Irish, Scottish, and English identities. Smith [1991], before the Maastricht Treaty which established the European community, admits that the regional cooperation of Europe, since the treaty of Rome in 1956, has resulted in the emergence of the European Community, but contrary to Delanty, he says that the European Identity "will not even approximate to the British or Belgian models" [Smith 1991, 170]. The post-national European identity is more than what Smith claims. Other authors regard European identity as a post-national identity which represents Europe's future with no nations. Rambour [2005, 3], at the time of the Failure of the Constitutional Treaty, quoting Delanty and Smith, argues that Delanty conceives Europe not as a political or cultural community or as a real society because he conceives nation states as strong. He [2005, 3] further calls Smith too as a strong supporter of nationalism who argues that European identity is not able to elicit the loyalty and mobilization that nationalism is able to do. As a result of this, according to Smith, the European identity "could only be weak, as it wouldn't be supported by the emotional background presented at the national level" [Rambour, M. 2005, 3].

Walkenhorst [2009, 15], when the Lisbon Treaty was ratified, records his personal belief about the post-national future of Europe when he says that European "identity model reflects a post-national and post-modern philosophy which is tailored for an age of 'global flattening', where ethnical, economic and cultural differences increasingly disappear". Jackobs, D. and Maier, R, [1998, 11], writing after the Maastricht Treaty, also give a post-national explanation of possible development of European identity: "a substantial European identity can only be achieved if it is based on a deracialised and deculturalised conception of European society, based on... constitutional patriotism". Valentini, Ch. [2005, 5], after the failure of the Constitutional Treaty, defines European identity as a post-national political identity: "European identity can be defined as a specific type of existing, or emerging, collective identity which is founded on the feeling of belonging to a certain entity". In the same work he explains the post-national nature of European identity by touching the exaltation of "feeling" based on civic rights and political norms as means of identification: "European identity is based on adherence to civic and political norms rather than ethno-cultural ties" [Valentini, Ch. 2005, 5].

Kaelberer [2004, 16] does not share such an optimism. Writing shortly before the failure of EU's Constitutional Treaty, he states: "Clearly, any form of a European identity would be quite different from the national identities of individual EU member states. For the foreseeable future, a European identity will most likely remain weaker than the respective national identities. There is little prospect for European identity to rival national identity anytime soon". Contrary to Rambour, Walkenhorst and other authors, he doesn't believe that the post-national era is coming soon in Europe. Similar with Kaelberer, White [2010, 178], in the time when the EU's member countries increased to 27, argues that: "Identity in Europe...is more complicated than some scholars make it out to be. If there is to be an identity shift in Europe it will be over decades, maybe even centuries, not months and years".

Oner upholds a relative more moderate view, neither pessimistic nor optimistic, with regards to the development of the

21

European identity. The author [Oner, 2004, 34], in the time of Constitutional Treaty, argues that national identities are going to remain strong in Europe when he says that: "It is highly unlikely that European identity replaces national one. It is more probable in Europe, people having multiple identities." Perhaps the idea of multiple identities given by Oner, similar to Delanty's pyramid of identities, that of the European identity developing alongside national identities in the form of multiple identities, is neither optimistic nor pessimistic predication of the European identity's development in the near future.

Another problem which leads to diverse and confused definitions of the European identity by scholars is the 'sui generis' nature of EU. As Smith [1991, 8] points out, it is the political unity which results in the creation of the political community. Hence, a 'sui generis' EU can only result in the generation of a 'sui generis' European identity. Wailer [1995, 268], before the Constitutional Treaty, describes this as: "The European Union, it is generally accepted, is not a state. The result is a description of oranges with a botanical vocabulary developed for apples". Another feature which makes European identity a 'sui generis' phenomenon are the consolidated national identities of Europe. The EU identity case, as a 'sui generis' one, is different from the case of U.S.A. which binds its people by the 'constitutional patriotism' and is even considered a nation though its citizens belong to diverse ethnic groups. Ethnically diverse groups in U.S.A. were bound by a constitution and values on whose foundation they constructed a nation-state, but the process of nation formation was easier in the US because its first newcomer citizens more often than not did not identify themselves on national bases when they came to live in US. On the contrary, the European identity is a project put in action at a time of consolidated national identities of EU-member states. This fact makes again European identity a 'sui generis' phenomenon.

To summarize, identities nowadays are dynamic and shift together with peoples' loyalty and economic incentives. Such a shift has been facilitated by peoples' multiple identities and loyalties. Thus, EU's single market and political unity consequently influence the adaption of the European identity as a collective identity of the European political community. The role of new developments in information and transportation technology to this end is indispensable in making communication between cultures possible thereby eroding bases on which national identities were once constructed. Nationalism is declining, opening thus the way to European identity and even to a world cosmopolitan identity. Because of the development of these new global factors "Many…argue, and point out that the world's societies of the 21st century will be completely mixed up, and while traditional identities will remain in place, they will lose their influence" [Thomas, D. Schult, Ch. Zuber, H. 2011, 1]. Ethnic and cultural ties will lose grounds. Human rights are gaining impetus but still national identities are strong. In conclusion, as Delanty [2005, 2] argues, all these will result in further evolution of the European identity in the shape of a pyramid of identities with European identity at the top. European identity, as we saw, comprises post-national elements (65%) combined with national elements. It is a western European continental sense of belonging to a European community. It is post-national identity combined with national elements whose evolution requires a constitution to serve as a social contract which will make Europeans loyal to the constitution. It requires a deeper integration of the EU and even a 'federation', a process which starts with the establishment of the constitution itself.

European identity and EU Constitutional Treaty

In our discussion on 'constitutional patriotism' [Chapter 1, 18-19], we argued that Constitution or similar provisions consolidate European identity by increasing people's loyalty toward the EU, thus enforcing the collective identity of European political community. Even in its failure, as we demonstrate in this chapter, the Constitution increased the consolidation degree of European identity through the enhancement of European public spheres. As we shall also investigate in this chapter, the consolidation degree of the European identity shall also contribute to the success of constitutional ratification. Hence, in this chapter we shall demonstrate that European identity and the Constitution need to develop simultaneously. The Switzerland case, as shall be argued on the bases of analogical reasoning, provides solid evidence thereupon.

The founding fathers of the European Union did not hesitate to speak about their aim, i.e. a European Federation. In 1950, in the establishment of the "Steel and Coal Community", they suggested that economic interdependence associated with the establishment of a High Authority would lead to a European Federation. Robert Schuman (1886-1963), a Frenchman born in Luxemburg, deeply influenced by his background in the French-German border and a first-hand witness of the calamities of ethnic divisions effected by World War II, through his internationally renowned Schuman Plan (May 09, 1950) deservedly considered amongst the founding fathers of the EU, seemed to be precisely aware of where this endeavour would eventually lead to: "The pooling of coal and steel production will immediately assure the establishment of common bases for economic development as a first step for the European Federation… By pooling basic industrial production and setting-up a new High Authority whose decisions will be binding on France, Germany and other member countries, these proposals will bring to reality the first solid groundwork for a European Federation vital to the preservation of world peace" [Schuman, R. 1950, 1]. In the establishment of the

'Coal and Steel Community', Schuman appreciated that the High Authority would function "as a first (mean) for the European Federation" [1950, 1]. At the beginning of the 21st century all the prerequisites set by the EU's founding fathers seemed to have been reached; hence, it seems to make sense for the EU to undertake the next step toward this plan, by the establishment of a European constitution.

On May 31, 2005, a couple of days after France rejected the European constitution, Gregston sarcastically scoffed at his World Press report: "The dream of a United Europe has shattered in France, the country where it was born" [Gregston, B. 2005]. Gergston apparently undermined that a Europe united by a Constitution is not merely a vision but a process through which the EU has to pass. This, however, is a long way, where debates about the distribution of power between EU and its member states are prominent and passes, as we shall demonstrate in this chapter, through the consolidation of the European identity, which, in its turn, shall leverage public support for the European constitution. Hence, a consolidated European identity means no spill-back for EU.

To delve into the nuts and bolts of this chapter, I have retrieved primary materials from the Eurobarometer, which publishes regular surveys of public opinion related with the European Union. The data published by the Eurobarometer are very important in understanding the degree of consolidation of the European identity and the support for the constitution. Then, in the method of analogical reasoning I shall contextualize the Swiss cases into the EU identity debate.

In this chapter we will present the figures showing the consolidation degree of the European identity in comparison to similar figures of national identities **[Table 2]**. These figures demonstrate that Europeans have a dual identity (a national identity and a European), thereby enabling them to shift their loyalty from the EU to their nation and vice-versa. In this frame we shall attempt to analyze the reasons behind the failure of the EU constitution's ratification in France and the debate between Habermas and Eurosceptics. It is demonstrated through the Swiss case, by way of analogical reasoning, that the EU Constitution and the civic nation (*demos*) have to develop simultaneously, an argument which has to be added to the debate between Habermas and Eurosceptics.

The initial hypothesis of this chapter was that there is a positive correlation between the level of consolidation of the European identity and the EU integration in general, hypothesis deduced from Smith's [1991, 8] theory of political community. As Smith [1991, 8] argues, the political unity creates its political community. This argument leads to the hypothesis that the more integrated the EU is the stronger the European identity becomes. The table presented in chapter 3 **[Table 4]** does not confirm this hypothesis, though, the absence of positive correlation might be interpreted on the grounds of insufficient available information about the consolidation degree of the European identity after the Constitutional Treaty. Still, as I shall demonstrate, the EU Constitution, even in its failure, enhances the consolidation of the European political community.

Nowadays, when the single market and common currency has been created and Europe has its own Parliament - the conditions that EU's Founding Fathers believed to lead to the European Federation - the next step toward the European Federation has to be the establishment of the European constitution. Though not the final step to European Federation, it was a mean in "inventing a new political form, something more than confederation but less than a federation" [Habermas, J, 2001, 5]. Three years before EU's attempt to ratify a Constitutional Treaty, Habermas [2001, 15] wondered: "Does Europe in its present shape meet the conditions necessary for the realization of such a design—that is: for the establishment, not simply of a confederation, but a federation of nation-states?"

The failure of the Constitutional Treaty (2005), attempted

three years after Habermas' question, showed that Europe was not ready for such a design. The outcome of the referendum on EU's Constitutional Treaty held in France and in Netherland on 29 May 2005 was disappointing. In France, 55% voted against of the constitution, while the percentage of those who voted likewise in the Netherland reached 62% [Kral, D. 2006, 1].

Even before this failed attempt, Habermas [2001, 15] noted that "Eurosceptics reject a shift in the basis of legitimation of the Union from international treaties to a European constitution with the argument, 'there is as yet no European people'. According to this view, what is missing is the very subject of a constituent process, the collective singular of 'a people' capable of defining itself as a democratic nation" [Habermas 2001, 15]. In his strong belief in 'constitutional patriotism', Habermas argued about the necessity of a post-national conceptualization of *demos* for the realization of a European Constitution. He [2011, 15] emphasized his post-national view of the *demos* by saying: "I have criticized this 'no-demos' thesis on both conceptual and empirical grounds" [2001, 15]. We can arguably claim that a post-national European *demos* in political/legal terms exists. Eurosceptics, on the other hand, assert that such European *demos* does not exist in ethno/cultural terms in the absence of a common European culture. The case of Switzerland, as we shall demonstrate, as well as the concrete EU plans to instill, foster and cultivate a common European culture will show that their argument is not really substantiated, though the raw fact that the constitution failed stands on their side. But, which were the reasons for the failure of the European constitution?

Vassallo [2007, 4] attributes the failure of the constitution in France to the long time between the announcement of the referendum and the voting, which gave time to the Opposition party to organize itself, presenting the European Constitution as conflicting national interests thereby turning it to a matter of high domestic politics. [Vassallo, F. 2007, 4]. The "No" camp (the opposition party) managed to shift the loyalty of the people who identified themselves first on national bases and then as Europeans. Their shift in loyalty, which affected their voting behavior, happened for reasons of national interest. "About one third of the voters cast their vote because of their general opinion on the social and economic situation in France" [Vassallo, F. 2007, 5]. Dinan [2010, 149] too, attributes the failure to the national interest. The opposition camp in France took advantage of the French fear of the economic integration as a reason to reject the constitution. French workers also feared the immigration from the east who could fill their jobs. "In Holland as in France, most of the dissatisfaction had little to do with the treaty itself. Clearly, the referendum had provided an opportunity for voters to express deep dissatisfaction with developments in their own counties" [2010, 150]. Ensnared between voting for someone else's interest, as the EU Constitution was viewed, and their own national interests, the French and the Dutch shifted their loyalty from the EU to their own country and rejected the Constitutional Treaty.

Statistical data retrieved from the Eurobarometer 62 (2004) and 64 (Spring and Fall 2005, 23-25), i.e. before, during and shortly after the EU Constitutional Treaty's failure provide noteworthy evidence of identification shift that influenced the results of the French and Dutch referenda [Table 2]. Data from the Eurobarometer are published in the official website of the European Commission and contain Public Opinion Analysis statistics about Europe. Data reported by Eurobarometer 62 (2004) on the degree of consolidation of the European identity one year before the constitutional ratification is condensed in table 2 below.

Table 2. % of citizens identifying themselves with a European identity vs National identity (2004)

European only	European & Nationality	Nationality & European	Nationality only
4%	7%	48%	37%

Source: Eurobarometer 62, 2004, 97.

The groups identified above indicate the personal identification of European citizens, as Europeans and/or members of their nation, and pinpoints the groups susceptible to identification shifts in the way discussed in Chapter 1 [17]. It is these groups' loyalty that influences their voting behaviour. As the table shows, in 2004, 4% of Europeans identified themselves only as Europeans, -- 7% identified themselves first as Europeans first and then on national bases, -- 48% identified themselves firstly on national bases, – while 37% identified themselves only on national grounds. The two groups of 7% and 48% who identified themselves as Europeans and on national bases pertain to European citizens with multiple identities **[Table 2]**. As argued in Chapter 1 [14-18], the loyalty of these groups can shift along with their identification from the European Union to their national state and vice versa, depending on their interest. Hence, the citizens of these two groups can sometimes behave as supporters of the Constitution, whereas, if the EU Constitution was viewed as conflicting national interest, the voting behavior can differ. 37% of the European populations who identified themselves only on national bases **[Table 2]** represent the people who might not have been in favour of the European constitution from the outset and, presumably, did not support it in the 2005 referenda. Eurobarometer 64 [2005, 23-25] **[Table 3]** reports that the percentage of Europeans who were at the time against the idea of the constitution varied between 23% and 21%, rather significantly lower than the rate of 37% who, after Table 2, identified themselves solely in national terms.

The total percentage of people who have some sense of being European is 59% (4% + 7% + 48% = 59%) [Table 2]. Eurobarometer 62 [149] reports that at the time of French referendum in May 2005, the support for the constitution in the EU level before the constitutional ratification was 61%, a percentage slightly higher than the percentage of people who were shown to have a sense of being Europeans (59%). Though the figure 61% shows a high percentage of people who could have voted in favour of the constitution, Eurobarometer 62 clarifies that "this result must not be seen as a voting intention in those countries that are considering or have scheduled a referendum on the Constitutional Treaty".

Six months after the failure of the constitution, Eurobarometer 64 [23-25] reports another shift in loyalty of Europeans: "In the Netherlands, the percentage of people who support the idea of a constitution has increased by 9 points from 53% to 62%. The percentage that opposes this idea has gone down from 38% to 34%. In France, favorable responses toward the constitution have increased by 7 points to 67%. This is accompanied by an equally large drop in unfavorable responses so that the percentage of people in France who disagree that the European Union should have a Constitution now stands at 21%" [Eurobarometer 64, 23-25; cf. **Table 3**].

The percentage of people who supported the idea of an EU constitution had not been increased only in France and Netherland but in most of European countries. In EU level the increase goes from 61% to 63% of Europeans. **Table 3** below shows the increase in percentage of people who supported the constitution. The data were taken in spring 2005 (Note: French voted the constitution on May 2005) and in autumn 2005 when the failure of the constitution was announced.

Table 3: Percentage of European citizens in favour of an EU Constitution by member-state and in total, classified in a decreasing scale.

State	Spring 2005	Autumn 2005	The increase	The decrease
AT	47%	49%	+2	
BE	76%	77%	+1	
CY	73%	72%		-1
CZ	44%	50%	+6	
DE	68%	74%	+6	
DK	42%	45%	+3	
EE	52%	49%		-3
EL	60%	68%	+8	
ES	63%	62%		-1
FI	47%	49%	+2	
FR	60%	67%	+7	
HU	78%	76%		-2
IE	54%	58%	+4	
IT	74%	70%		-4
LU	63%	69%	+6	

LV	56%	57%	+1	
MT	50%	60%	+10	
NL	53%	62%	+9	
PL	61%	60%		-1
PT	59%	63%	+4	
SE	38%	44%	+6	
SI	76%	74%		-2
SK	60%	64%	+4	
UK	43%	46%	+3	
EU	61%	63%	+2	

Source: Eurobarometer 64, 2005, p. 23-25. Highlights by the author.

The increase in the percentage of people who supported the idea of a constitution can also be read as an increase of their awareness in the importance of the constitution. There is no evidence that this happened because Europeans regretted what the French and Dutch did in polls. Summing up the percentage of groups in **Table 2** who identified themselves as European, either exclusively (4%) or as part of their multiple identities (7% and 48%), we can conclude that the percentage of European citizens who could be in favour of a European constitution in 2004 was 59%. Eurobarometer [62, 149] reports that the percentage of Europeans in favor of the constitution was 61%; i.e. 2% more than the percentage of people identifying themselves in terms of their European identity. A year after, in 2005, and after the failure of the EU Constitutional Treaty ratification, this percentage reached 63% (i.e. +4%). A difference of 4% cannot be attributed to any sort of marginal error. A similar situation is reported by Eurobarometer 71 [2009, 34]. The percentage of European identity increased from 71% in 2008 to 74% in 2009, the time when the Lisbon Treaty entered into force. How are we to understand this difference and from what group does the increased support to the EU Constitution come?

We suggest that the build-up in the European citizens' awareness of the importance of an EU constitution is a result of European public spheres regenerated in the course of voting for the Constitutional Treaty, a process which turned some of the people who identified themselves only on national terms (37%) in favor of the constitution. As Risse and Grabowsky [2008, 1] argue, a: "public sphere plays an important role for the emergence of a common identity", which, in our case, seems to have influenced in the consolidation of the European identity and the subsequent support to the EU Constitution. Debating the constitution in the European public spheres emphasizes its importance. Such debates closely connect the people with their governments, thereby creating political communities. Risse and Grabowsky [2008, 7] argue that "The more we debate issues, the more we engage each other in our public discourse – and the more we actually create political communities".

Nation-states have consolidated their public spheres in the course a long period of time and this has contributed to the consolidation of their national identities. The evolution of European public spheres in a similar way is a difficult task because Europeans lack a common language through which they can communicate with each other. These difficulties notwithstanding, in whatever degree European public spheres evolve, they contribute in the consolidation of the European public even when they compete with national identities, as this 4% increase, noted in Table 3 and pooled from the 37% of the people who in 2004 identified themselves only on national grounds, indicates.

Risse and Grabowsky [2008, 8] are convinced about the

33

effect of European public spheres: "overall, it can be stated that not only a European public sphere is emerging but that there is some evidence regarding a collective European identity as being constructed in the course of transnational debates about European issues of common concern to Europeans". The most striking example and perhaps the case which verifies the strong existence of European public spheres, is the rebellion of EU citizens against the US unilateral action during the Iraq war, which was in contradictions with "soft security" agenda of EU foreign policy. In 2003, European citizens filled the streets of Europeans capitals like Paris, Berlin, London and other European capitals. Their protest was against the attack of Iraq by USA. The demonstrations were among the largest in the continent history [Cottey 2007, 58]. This case also constitutes evidence of the consolidated European identity and of the role of European public spheres influencing and supporting the "soft-security" agenda of the EU's foreign policy.

Apart from the efforts to create and enhance European public spheres, EU has created a variety of programs to influence directly in the consolidation of European identity as nationalism did. EU has its anthem, its flag and the European Day. EU has its most important symbol; the euro. In similarity with national projects, EU has been driven by elites. EU has created programs which encourage cultural exchange like: **Erasmus, Leonardo Da Vinci, Tempus** and **Comenius.** The top-bottom approaches of creating their *demos* are both the same. [Clinpoe 2008, 7]. Furthermore these programs are named after famous figures of Europe who are able to play the role that national heroes played in the creation of their nation. Clinpoe [2008, 7] argues that their goal is "to create a sense of solidarity by appealing … to personalities that have universal, but also European … value". Other programs created by the EU are: **SOCRATES** which improves education through foreign language learning [Socrates Programme], **INTERREG** which encourages knowledge transfer to develop economies at regional scales and to protect the environment [Interreg IVC], the **European Observatory Records** which gathers data about EU activities [European Commission II], **IPA** which supports the candidate and potential candidate countries [European Commission III] etc.

As we shall demonstrate below, apart from creating and enhancing public spheres, a constitution, once established, creates and consolidates political communities in a variety of other ways. Constitution serves as a contract which unites people. It serves as "a call for a civic patriotism" [Monnet, J. Schuman, R. 2005, 2]. Citizens are bound to each other through this social contract. Monet and Schuman [2005, 2], the founding fathers of EU, argue that: "Citizens accept institutions as legitimate if they can be justified by some kind of social contract. So far, these principles have been mainly applied in the national arena, since there are few instances in which the EU establishes a social contract with its citizens; treaties (which have been serving as a constitution for EU) are not recognized as such". The establishment of a European constitution will serve as a social contract which shall function as bond amongst Europeans and will facilitate the acceptability of EU institutions as legitimate by European citizens. Treaties which serve as Constitution for EU, cannot replace the role of the contract that the Constitution plays to its citizens.

Constitutions have served as social contract also used by nation-states; my argument, though, is that its role is not part of nationalist theories. 'Constitutional patriotism' too has been used by states to foster their national identity. US is an example in which a state seceded to create its nation through the use of 'constitutional patriotism'. As Beta [2012, 1] argues: "An important part of the patriotism of the Americans is 'constitutional patriotism': pride their constitution and civic institutions. The European Union... should foster a sense of 'European identity' by adopting a constitution, in which every citizen of EU can take pride".

In Chapter 1 we elaborated on the concept of 'Constitutional patriotism'; in this section, we shall demonstrate how its theory is relevant, applicable and appropriate in the European context. Delanty [1996, 2] argues that "appeals to the cultural heritage of Europe, to a geographical territory, to language, to a dominant ethnic group can only be divisive, demarcating Europeans from each other as well as setting them off from the extra-European world". Only the 'constitutional patriotism' can create the sense of solidarity and build a new collective identity for Europe. He further argues that a post-national identity for Europe based on 'constitutional patriotism' "is the only kind of national identity compatible with the requirements of a multicultural society" [Delanty 1996, 2]. With the exception of the term 'national identity', which I do not see fit for the European identity, his argument, i.e. that a post-national identity is the only identity for the multicultural society of Europe, appears to be very convincing. Writing only four years after the Maastricht treaty, three years after the establishment of the single market in 1993 and well before the Euro-currency was launched, the same author argued that: "something like a post-national identity might be a suitable model for European identity in the twenty-first century" [1996, 2], an idea which is well recognized today in the twenty-first century and strongly advocated by such scholars as Rambour [2005] and Guler [2011].

While the approach of scholars mentioned above was by and large theoretical, the case of Switzerland promises to provide a unique example of how 'constitutional patriotism' leads to the establishment of an identity with post-national elements for a multicultural society; by way of analogical reasoning, the Swiss paradigm can arguably be inferred to the EU case. Switzerland is composed of several communities, mainly French, Italian and German. Its people speak four languages [Swissuniversity. ch], just like the case of EU citizens. The Swiss case is very similar to the EU in regard of origin. Just like the 'Steel and Coal community' from which the EU originated, the Swiss unification started with the agreement for mutual defense signed during the 13th century by its three cantons Uri, Unterwalden and Schwyz, which today form the central Switzerland [Stojanivic 2003, 48]. Alike the 'Coal and Steel' agreement signed between Germany and French to settle the disputes over Alsace and Lorraine [European navigator 2010, 3], the initial purpose of the Swiss agreement was mutual defense. The alliance signed in 1291 between these three communities of the central Alps was for perpetual mutual assistance in case of war [Swissuniversity. Ch]. Like the 'Coal and Steel Community' later incorporated the entire Europe [CCLL, 2010, 4], so did the initial community of Switzerland which enlarged and incorporated other cantons most of which joined the union in the 14th century. First, the alliance proved to be valid when they resisted the Hapsburg attack. As a result, other communities joined and others were conquered [Swissuniversity. ch]. These communities are: Lucerne which joined the union in 1332, Zurich in 1351, Glarus in 1352, Zug in 1352, Bern in 1353), St. Gallen in1451, Appenzell in 1452, Schaffhausen in 1459 etc [Stojanovic 2003, 48]. In a closer resemblance with the EU, Stojanovic [2003, 48] calls it a "union of sovereign states".

Differently from the EU, the Swiss nation emerged during the time of Napoleon Bonaparte, when nationalism first emerged in Europe. Napoleon's invasion to Switzerland in 1798 caused political changes. The 'Helvetic Republic', the former name for Switzerland, became very centralized, like the French Republic [2003, 49]. The Swiss nation from the outset comprised post-national elements. When Napoleon invaded Switzerland, he created the first Swiss institutions. Inhabitants held the same rights and duties. Like the EU, it was the existence of the Swiss state which engineered the formation of the common Swiss identity. Though a constitution was not yet reality at the time, we can say that there were these post-national elements like civic rights and duties which enabled for the first time the emergence of the Swiss identity and nation approximately five centuries after this community was first created in the 13th century. The creation of the Swiss state together with post-national elements such as civic rights "provided the bases for the creation of a distinct Swiss civic identity among the population and differentiated it from neighbouring countries often akin in language and/or religion…The Helvetic Republic played an essential role in the process of nation-building in Switzerland. It did so by creating the institutions of a modern state based on the rule of law and on the protection of basic rights and liberties to which all citizens were equally entitled" [Stojanovic 2003, 53].

Though the Swiss identity and nation had began to take shape at the end of the 18th century and the beginning of the 19th century, Stojanovic [2003, 55] argues that the Swiss nation was not completely developed in the time when the Swiss constitution was established in 1848. "Did the Swiss 'nation' exist in the first half of the 19th century? The question is undoubtedly badly formulated because the nation-building process was still in progress" [Stojanovic 2003, 55]. The constitution, which is considered as an essential element of post-national theory and the core of 'constitutional patriotism', was missing in that period. The conclusion that we can draw from this is that the existence of a fully developed Swiss *demos* and nation were not indispensable for the establishment of the constitution, as Eurosceptics argue in the case of the EU - but on contrary, the constitution, established in 1848 in Switzerland, assisted in the formation of the Swiss identity and *demos*. Stojanovic [2003, 61] even considers the establishment of the constitution in 1848 as the point where the Swiss nation began to take shape in cultural terms: "As a matter of fact, the year 1848 appears as a symbolic dividing line between the political relevance of the political and cultural definition of 'nation'", a topic which goes beyond the aim of this essay. The Swiss case demonstrates that the constitution can be established in cases where the collective identity and nation are not fully created but are in their formative process. This also demonstrates that the Eurosceptics' claim that an European constitution cannot be created because 'there is as yet no

European people' [quoted in Habermas 2001, 15] is not reasonable. On the contrary, it is the constitution which further develops the collective identity in multicultural societies such as the Switzerland and EU and, as Stojanovic [2003, 61] argues, in the cultural definition of the Swiss 'nation'.

The EU integration process has always been characterized by debates over the distribution of power. Some politicians defend the creation of a federation with centralized power whereas others support states' sovereignty. The federalists, who come mostly from small states of Europe, support the further integration of EU until it reaches the federal stage, generating thus a strong political and military power. [Jackobs, D. Maier, R, 1998, 10]. Similar debates occurred upon the establishment of the Swiss Constitution in 1848 and of the US Constitutions in 1787, two countries which have succeeded in creating nations at the absence of common ethnicity. On one side there were the cantonal defenders (in the Switzerland) and of the state rights (in US) against the federalists who were pro of the federation [Stojanovic 2003, 59]. In Switzerland the situation was aggravated to such an extent that the debate ended up in a civil war in November 3, 1847. It was a short war with 86 victims and 500 wounded and ended with the victory of the federal army [Switzerland's History].

Another debate in the establishment of Switzerland's constitution was over the concept of the "nation". Throughout the Swiss Constitution, the Swiss were called "citizens" rather than "nationals". [Switzerland 2010, 6]. The reason for this was that the idea that a plurilingual nation could exist was unaccepted and even unimaginable [Stojanovic 2003, 61]. Stojanovic [2003, 61] touches the core of the debate on nationhood with these questions: "What is the nation? Is Switzerland a nation?" [2003, 61]. Constructivists argue that nations are imagined; hence, they can be constructed [Anderson 1991, 10]. According to this view, Switzerland is a

39

nation.

Considering that the European Constitution's ratification failed in 2005 because, first, - it was in conflict with national interest in fear of immigrants taking work places from nationals, and, second, - European identity was weaker than national identities, we can anticipate that the chances for a European constitution to be eventually ratified are not lost. The establishment of the European constitution would require a better off Eastern Europe (an Eastern Europe with fewer emigrants) and a stronger European identity. These are exactly what the EU is doing nowadays in its right track. In addition to the Lisbon Treaty (2007), EU is working on strengthening the economy of eastern countries and at the same time, is funding programmes to enhance and promote the consolidation of European identity. To conclude, the chances for a European constitution are not lost, since there are better prospects in the future.

To summarize this chapter, we can say that the failure of the EU constitution in 2004, its public support at the rate of 61% [Table 3] as well as the percentage of people against it 21% [Eurobarometer 64, 25], implies a low degree of consolidation of the European identity. 92% of the European citizens (37% + 48% + 7% = 92%) [Table 2] identified themselves, exclusively or not, as nationals of a member-state, while the percentage of European citizens identifying themselves, exclusively or not, as EU citizens was only 59% (4% + 7% + 48% = 59%) [Eurobarometer 62, 149; cf. **Table 2**]. These figures show that the degree of consolidation of the European identity compared to national identity was low in the time of Constitutional Treaty (2005).

Eurobarometer reports indicate a loyalty shift of Europeans in favor of the constitution after the failure of the constitutional ratification with an increase in percentage from 61% to 63% in EU level [Eurobarometer 64, 24; cf. Table 3]. This figure goes beyond the degree of consolidation of the European identity indicated in **Table 2** (59%). This 4% increase may indicate that some people who previously identified only on their national bases (37%) turned in favor of the constitution. The increase in percentage of those in support of the constitution can be attributed to the enhancement of public spheres before and after the ratification process. This suggests that, even in its failure, the constitution contributed in the further consolidation of the European identity through public spheres. Eurobarometer 71 [34] reports that in the time of Lisbon Treaty (2007 – 2009), the percentage of people who had a sense of being Europeans increased from 71% in 2008 to 74% in 2009 and national identities decreased from 25% to 22%. It is the argument of this chapter that the existence of a Constitution would further the consolidation degree of the European identity through 'constitutional patriotism' as well as through other means like public spheres. So, it seems that that the European identity and the ratification of a European constitution are intercommunicating containers, where the degree of consolidation of the European identity affects the success of the constitutional ratification and, on the other hand, the constitution affects the further consolidation of the European identity as a collective identity.

The European identity and National Identities in EU member States

On June 2008, J. Bismarck, sarcastically scoffed in the title of his World Press report: "Why PIGS can't fly" [Bismarck, 2008, 1]. His principal point was that northern Europe economies perform better than southern European economies because they benefited from the increase of the bulk of exports in Eastern Europe and Asia: "Those at risk are the PIGS—Portugal, Italy, Greece and Spain—who earned their nickname by staying stuck as their nimbler competitors revived export and job growth by venturing abroad" [2008, 1]. The reason he uses the term "PIGS", which also appears to be and the answer to his title's question, seems to be the failed attempts of Southern European economies to benefit from expanding their exports volumes in Northern Africa and even invest there. The title of this article is pejorative and rather offensive for southern countries of Europe, which, contrary to how Bismarck treats them, possessed the wealth as well as the wisdom of Europe in the past. European civilization originates from the ancient civilization of Creta and Micenas situated in Greece. Roman Empire (Italy) represents the common European history. Portugal was among the first European countries which explored the seas. Spain was the biggest European empire in middle ages.

The use of the mocking term "PIGS" in this article implies the existence of national feelings and consciousness which support the view that nationalism is strong in Europe. From the article, and more specifically from the use of the term "PIGS", we can deduce that northern European countries are represented as "We" or "Us", a term which comprises northern region of Europe represented as a single unity with approximately the same economic level. On the other hand, the south is presented as the "Others" who share similar economic and structural problems and are excluded from the northern region of Europe [Chapter 1]. In the article we see "inclusionary" and "exclusionary" feelings of the national identity; feelings which indicate who belongs in the group (nation) and who does not. Smith considers the division of Europe into regions as the strength of nationalism able to spread national sentiments and attitudes beyond their nation [1991, 168]. In doing so, he [169] argues that regions are the way in which states entrench their national sentiments and consciousness and even spread them beyond the boundaries of their nation: "Contrary to much current thinking, it is the very political configuration of states into wider regional systems that helps to entrench the power of the nation and fan the flames of nationalism everywhere" [Smith 1991, 169].

On the other hand, the use of the term "PIGS" in this article demonstrates also the emergence of a new identity which transcends the boundaries of traditional nation-states, resulting in the erosion of national identities as the only or the dominant means of identification. Eurobarometer 62 [2004, 1004] reports that, at the time of Constitutional Treaty, 88% of Europeans felt attached to their region. Eurobarometer 71 [2009, 37], held in the time of Lisbon Treaty, reports that the percentage of European citizens who felt attached to their region increased from 88% to 91%. Special Eurobarometer [2010, 70] reports that this percentage goes back to 88%, but with an increase by 2% of respondents who felt very attached to their region. This new regional identity, though similar with national identities even in their emotional configuration, influences in the erosion of national identities as the only or the dominant mean of identification. Nations are no more the largest communities through which people identify themselves; instead, nowadays larger communities have emerged in regional or larger levels. The existence of these other identities alongside national identities in the form of multiple identities erodes the role of national identities as the only or the dominant means of identification. Oner [2004, 33] argues that in the structure of a "Europe of Regions"

43

rather than a Europe composed of nation-states, "nation-states may dissolve in time". His view goes beyond the idea of a declining nationalism in Europe, as the author dares to argue that nations may dissolve in Europe.

In this chapter I shall first discuss the factors which result in the erosion of nationalism. I shall continue with Smith's criticisms about the idea of supersession or replacement of national identities by European identity. Next, I shall present Smith's three arguments about the strength of nationalism and of the impossibility of supersession or replacement of national identities by European identity. After presenting this dispute over the decline and strength of nationalism, I shall demonstrate the table which shows the consolidation degree of European identity as well as of the national identities in Europe. Based on the argument of the first chapter, i.e. that differently from national identities European identity is a post-national identity as well as on scholars' conclusion about the supersession of national identities by European identity, we shall argue that even if national identities cannot be superseded they can co-exist with European identity.

Jackobs and Maier [1998, 6] argue that human and civic rights have resulted in the erosion of national identities. These two elements - the most important elements in consolidating the post-national identity in Europe - are, perhaps, the prime factors which have resulted in the erosion of the national identities. These rights are no longer linked to nationhood. They are not granted to the individual as a member of the nation, but are granted as a human being. The importance of human rights has even replaced nationhood in political discourses [Jackobs and Maier 1998, 6]. Civic rights granted by institutions as European Court of Justice and European Parliament have eroded nation-states, though, as this chapter argues, they have not resulted in a full replacement or supersession of national identities.

Other causes for the erosion of nation-states, hand in hand with civic rights, are: the EU as a supra-national entity, globalization factors, cosmopolitanism and immigration. Rex [1996, 2] maintains that these factors have resulted in the erosion of nationalism:

> "Nation states find themselves belonging to supra-national entities like the European Union, or more generally caught up in a process of globalization involving international economic institutions and international media images; on the other they have had to face an intense process of immigration by minority groups with their own forms of culture and social organization. In these circumstances the established nations have been forced to ask whether they have a distinct identity of their own which is challenged by the forces of globalization and migration. The new nationalism is essentially a culture of resistance to these forces" [1996, 1].

In the last sentence Rex [1996, 1] considers the new nationalism as a resurgent force with which nations resist these forces. The decline of nationalism is accepted and by Delanty [1996, 2] but, contrary to Rex, he conceives the new nationalism as a product of the decline of nationalism rather than a resistance force. As a response to Rex, Delanty [1996, 2] argues that: "The new nationalism is.....more a product of the decline of nationalism as a dominant frame of identification than a new and resurgent force. In fact the new nationalism is closely related to the decline of nation-state as the dominant normative reference point for people today". The decline of national identities as "dominant frame of identification" [1996, 2], as we shall demonstrate at the end of this chapter, represents the main and perhaps the only decline of national identities, a decline which has resulted because of globalization, cosmopolitanism and supra-national entities like EU.

As argued in chapter 1, globalization stresses the role of communication between different cultures through information technology which results in the diminishing role of nationalism as well as in the creation of a global culture [Sindic, D. 2008, 1].

Based on the communication between cultures through information technology as well as on effects that supra-national organizations, such as the EU, have on nation-states' sovereignty, globalization strives for the creation of a global culture which results in the erosion of nationalism [Sindic 2008, 1]. Huntington [1993, 360] also argues that "the process of economic modernization and societal change through-out the world are separating people from longstanding local identities. They also weaken the nation state as a source of identity".

As I showed in Chapter 1, cosmopolitanism suggests that we belong to the whole world not to part of it; it presupposes that we are citizens of the world and emphasizes the idea of a "world state" where people are all equal. Cosmopolitanism means to be free from national ideas and prejudices. "Cosmopolitanism considers the case of a world society governed according to the principles of human rights and justice" [Rambour, 2005, 4]; a world without nations. Cosmopolitanism creates a shared identity between people of different nation, though in the form of multiple identities, which results in reduction of the likelihood of war, in a larger cooperation, as well as in the erosion of national identities as the dominant source of identification.

Though we mentioned most of the factors which influenced in the decline of nationalism, we must also say that some of them, like internet, can also have the opposite effect, too. Internet strengthens the relations of members of a nation and it can be used by nationals to strengthen nationalism. Besides internet there further are other points through which, as we shall detail below, Smith [1991] criticizes the idea that national identities can be superseded or replaced by European identity.

First, we have to say that Smith [1991, 155] too, accepts the emergence of the global culture and argues that "only continental cultures, ultimately a single global culture, can fulfill the requirements of a post-industrial knowledge-based society" [1991, 155], but his criticism is that even the creation of the global culture and of the cosmopolitan identity cannot lead to the supersession of national identities.

> "A growing cosmopolitanism does not in itself entail the decline of nationalism; the rise of regional culture areas does not diminish the hold of national identities. As I said at the outset, human beings have multiple collective identifications, whose scope and intensity will vary with time and place. There is nothing to prevent individuals from identifying with Flanders, Belgium and Europe simultaneously, and displaying each allegiance in the appropriate context.... It is, in fact, quite common, and very much what one would expect in a world of multiple ties and identities" [Smith 1991, 175].

His second criticism relates to the emotional configuration that the global culture lacks. The post-modern global culture, which Smith [1991, 158] calls "a pastiche of parodied styles and themes" would differ from all "previous (national) cultures not only in its worldwide diffusion but also in the degree of its self-consciousness and self-parody...Unlike previous cultural imperialisms, which were rooted in an ethnic time and place of origin, the new global culture is universal and timeless. Being eclectic, it is indifferent to place or time. It is fluid and shapeless...It boasts no history or histories; the folk motifs it uses are quarried for surface decoration of a present and future-oriented 'scientific' and technical culture. It is also a fundamentally artificial culture. Its pastiche is capricious and ironical; its effects are carefully calculated; and it lacks any emotional commitment to what is signified" [Smith 1991, 158]. His argument, that the new global culture differs from national cultures, seems right. National cultures were rooted in the common origin; they boasted the history of their nation. Global culture lacks these elements.

47

The fore mentioned points criticism lead Smith to maintain unswerving conviction about the role and strength of present national identities. He submits three arguments to argue about the strength of nationalism and the impossibility of supersession of national identities by European identity. The strongest point appears to be the emotional inspiration and mobilization that nationalism is able to erect.

Smith's [1991, 160] first argument about the strength of nationalism, which implies an enhanced role for nowadays national identities, equalizes the emotional appealing of nationalism with the role religion played in the past. In a way, he argues, nationalism replaces religion: "Identification with the 'nation' in a secular era is the surest way to surmount the finality of death and ensure a measure of personal immortality" [Smith 1991, 160]. Hayes, C. [2016] also assesses that nationalism in European countries has substituted religion with nationalism "over the past two centuries".

The motive which lead to the superstition of the religion by nationalism, at least in some European countries, is the strong national feeling in Europe. Similar to the way 'civic nations' are formed, European countries embodied divine elements to the symbols of nationalism e. g., flag, monuments, constitution, national heroes etc. Second, an appeal on the common origin was conducted (first by Napoleon) in order to strengthen national feelings. Such divinity embodied to the flag, monuments, national heroes and constitution, combined with the appeal on the common origin, resulted in the superstition of religion by the nationalism.

As Smith [1991, 160] insinuates, European Identity is not going to replace religion. Instead, as in USA, European Identity is going to create its civil religion, which, alike nationalism, does imply the divinity of the flag, monuments, constitution, national heroes etc., but, rather than the superstition of the religion by nationalism, civil religion implies an equalization between religion and nation, as in the USA. Such equalization between religion and nation will create religious harmony in the same way it did in the

USA which is well known for its religious harmony. Religious harmony and nationalism and the relations between the two shall be treated in details by us in another work.

His second argument about the strength of nationalism is that the common history and destiny with which nationalism creates bonds amongst the nation's members, as well as other means of reinforcing a collective identity, are brilliantly used by nationalists to date. "The nation can boast a distant past, even where much of it must be reconstructed or even fabricated. Even more important, it can offer a glorious future similar to its heroic past…So the primary function of national identity is to provide a strong 'community of history and destiny' to save people from personal oblivion and restore collective faith" [Smith 1991, 161].

Smith's third argument [1991, 162] is about the ideal of fraternity produced by nationalism: "A third function of national identity is the prominence it gives to fraternity, realizing the ideal of fraternity". His statement about the prevalence of fraternity among members of a nation is a strong point of present national identities but, we have to add here that it is not the perfect type of fraternity. A strong emphasis on common history, language, and origin produces minority groups. Within the population of a nation-state defining its nationalism on the common origin and ethnicity, as is the case of European nation-states, there are other groups with a different ethnicity considered as minority groups in hold of these states' citizenship. Post-national identity, on the other hand, does not create these minority groups. It unites all people to the constitution.

Among the strongest points of nationalism is what Risse and Grabowsky [2008, 1] argued that the EU still lacked at the time of Lisbon Treaty; the support that the affected citizens offer to their state. Smith [1991, 171] says that nationalism provides this support as well as sense of pride for masses and the vision of political solidarity which "command popular assent and elicit popular enthusiasm".

Which are the roots for such strong emotional appeal that nationalism is capable of generating, which may even cause a replacement of religion by nationalism? Smith (1990, 20-32) argues that when nationalism first appeared in Europe in the time of French Revolution was inspired by the Enlightenment principles. The emotional appeal and mass mobilization it created was generated by appealing to human rights and common territory. The US case demonstrates that such form of nationalism (i. e., appealing on human rights and common territory) is capable of creating a civic nation which is capable of generating emotional appeal even in the absence of the common origin. As the USA case demonstrates, such form of nationalism (i. e., civic nation) is even capable of equating nationalism with religion.

Smith [1991] argues that in some Eastern European countries, including Albania, emerged a new form of nationalism. The elite in some Eastern European countries appealed on the common origin and their right to the inherited territory in their efforts in raising national awareness and mobilizing the masses. They trumpeted that the territory in which they lived was inherited from their ancestors. This justified the right over the territory where they lived as well as their independence.

Albanian's elite (i. e., Rilindasit) successfully managed to raise national feelings by appealing only to the common origin and their right to the inherited territory. The mass mobilization they generated even constrained European countries to break their agreement of the Treaty of ST. Stephen (1878) and grant Albania the independence in 1912.

In addition to the rise of national feelings, the Albanian elites (Rilindasit) even managed to equalize religion with nationalism, as the USA which boasts the equalization they make between religion and nation. Nowadays Albanian academics still talk of the equalization of religion with nationalism in Albania terming it as the 'Binomial Religion Nation'. We can conclude that the common origin and the right to the inherited territory can be considered as a component of nationalism which alone is capable of arising national feelings and manages to mobilize masses and even in generating equalization between nationalism and religion.

Smith [1991] admits that for Europe - whose nations had a common origin too - this was a new form of nationalism. Napoleon used common origin in the consolidation of the French nation. Nazis further deepened the argument on common origin by manipulating and transforming common origin into the superiority of the Aryan race which should also be kept clean. Doing so, they added a second doze to the consolidation of their national identity. Two forms of nationalism, which independently could arise national feelings and even equate the nation with the religion, would lead to stronger emotional appeal and to what Hayes (2016) calls a substitution of religion by nationalism.

Table: 4. The percentage of European citizens identifying themselves as: i) European; ii) primarily European and secondary nationals; iii) Primarily nationals and secondarily European; iv) and exclusively nationals of their own EU member state in the various developmental stages of the EU.

Year	EU integration Development (12 member states)	Europe an only	Europe an & Nation ality	Nationalit y & European	Nationali ty only
1992	**Maastricht treaty is signed.**	4	7	**48**	**38**
1993	Maastricht Treaty comes into force. **The single market is created.**	4	7	45	40
1994		7	**10**	46	**33**
1995	Three new countries join the EU. (15 member countries)	5	6	46	40
1996		5	6	40	46
1997	Amsterdam treaty is signed.	5	6	40	45
1998		5	6	41	44
1999	Amsterdam Treaty comes into force. 11 EU member countries adopt the Euro.	4	7	43	43

Year	Event				
2000	Nice Treaty was signed.	4	8	45	41
2001	Laeken European Council. It opened the way for the Convention of the Constitution.	3	6	44	44
2002	**Euro is launched in a 12th EU member states.**	3	7	**49**	**38**
2003	The draft of the European Constitution is completed. Nice Treaty comes into force.	3	7	47	40
2004	**Ratification of the European Constitution begins.** 10 new countries join the EU. (25 member states)	4	7	**48**	37
2008	**The Lisbon Treaty is in ratifying process.**		71		**25**
2009	**Lisbon Treaty entered into force.**		74		22

Sources: Eurobarometer 50. (1999, 59); Eurobarometer 53. (2000, 80); Eurobarometer 54. (2000, 13); Eurobarometer 56. (2001, 13); Eurobarometer 58. (2002, 28); Eurobarometer 60. (2003, 27); Eurobarometer 62. (2004, 97); Eurobarometer 71. (2009, 34).

The percentage of European citizens identifying themselves as such either exclusively or complementary has remained virtually unaltered from the Maastricht Treaty (1992) to the Constitutional

Treaty (2004). The percentage of European citizens identifying themselves as such either exclusively or complementary was 59% in 1992 and remained 59% in 2004. National identities have not declined during this period. In spite of the fact that the Euro (the key-symbol of the European identity) was launched in 2002, the percentage of European citizens identifying themselves as such either exclusively or complementary continues to stay still (59%). The increase in the percentage of European identity to 71% and 74% is reported during the Lisbon Treaty (2008-2009), the treaty which replaced the constitution. It seems that the emotional significance represented to the constitution has more influence than the Euro, which, after being introduced in the Maastricht Treaty, seems not to have any effect as a symbol at all.

Smith's overall conclusion is that, though global culture and cosmopolitanism are emerging, they cannot supersede national identities which continue to trigger a strong emotional appeal; something that global culture and cosmopolitanism lack. Based on this, Smith [1991, 176] argues that national identity "is likely to continue to command humanity's allegiances for a long time to come, even when other larger-scale but looser forms of collective identity emerge alongside national ones". A similar conclusion is also reached and by Oner [2004, 30] at the time of the Constitutional Treaty, who conveys the same ideas in his words: "If political community is to be created within the EU, these kinds of emotional elements have to be used, as we see in the nation state model". His conclusion does not indicate only that nationalism has stronger emotional elements, but also argues for the need to incorporate these emotional elements to the European identity. The constitution, serving as a mean of inspiring people through the 'constitutional patriotism' can also serve as a source in which people can take pride and embody the same emotional elements to European identity as national identities do. The evolution of such emotional elements will create popular assent and support for the EU, of the sort that Risse and Grabowsky [2008, 1] argue that the EU currently lacks. US is the example in which the state was successful in creating a nation through 'constitutional patriotism' as well as in embodying emotional mobilization and popular assent to its citizens.

The question that Sindic [2008, 7] raised with regard to European identity versus national identities of Europe is "how much the process of European integration and attempts at building a sense of European identity has actually led to or will lead to a decline in national (and British) identity". Sindic's [2008, 9] response is:

> "As regard to the future, it is possible, of course, that European identity will gain strength over time in the next decades….Moreover, there are strong reasons to doubt that it will replace or supersede national identities in the near future…whilst it has been argued that the development of a European identity does not generally act like a zero-sum game,… It may nevertheless require its re-definition… the possibility of promoting a stronger sense of European identity would depend on re-defining either national or European identity so as to make them more compatible".

Their compatibility was dealt in chapter 1. In this unit, we shall investigate what their compatibility means in everyday life, what Europeans say about the co-existence of these two identities and what exactly happens between them. Eurobarometer 38 [1992, 45], a survey held in the 12 EU member-states at the time of the Maastricht Treaty, reported that 23% of Europeans believed at the time that national identities would disappear and would be replaced by European identity, whereas 63% believed that these two identities are compatible and can co-exist. Contrary to what 23% of Europeans believed in that time, Eurobarometer 71 [2009, 36], held in the time of Lisbon Treaty, reports that national identities had not disappeared after 17 years had elapsed from 1992 to 2009. It reports that 94% of Europeans shared the national identity of their country whereas 5% did not. This figure (94%) opposes the claim that national identities would disappear and would be replaced by the European identity. On the other hand, the same Eurobarometer 71 report [2009, 34] also records that the percentage of the percentage of European citizens identifying themselves as Europeans either exclusively or complementary had increased from 59% in 2004 to 74% in 2009, when the Lisbon Treaty entered into force **[Table 3]**. Since the percentage of national identities had not decreased, whereas, on the other hand, the percentage of European citizens identifying themselves as such either exclusively or complementary had increased, we can deduce that the European identity has developed alongside national identities in the form of multiple identities without replacing national identities or conflicting them, a view which maintains that European identity and national identities are compatible, as 63% of Europeans believed in 1992.

In conclusion we can say that European identity, assisted by the inconspicuous erosion of national identities, has developed alongside national identities in the form of multiple identities. By "erosion" here I mean the weakening role of national identities as the only or the dominant mean of identification with larger groups, a role it used to play in the past. This erosion of national identities has been facilitated by several factors.

The first factor which has led to the erosion of national identities is the creation of the European political community. European nations are no more the largest groups or communities through which people can identify with. Other identities have emerged nowadays, like the European identity, through which people can identify themselves with these larger communities like the European political community. National identities are no more the only means of identification.

The other factors which have led to the erosion of national identities are: human and civic rights, cosmopolitanism and globalization. Human and civic rights are no longer linked to nation-states but, instead, are linked to supra-national organizations and entities like the EU. Cosmopolitanism produces a world identity shared by different nations, an identity which erodes the dominant role of national identities. Communication between cultures results in the creation of a global culture as well as in the erosion of nationalism. Immigrants bring their cultures to other countries where they conglomerate with the dominant culture of the nations where they live. These cultural exchanges have resulted in the amalgamation of cultures whose result has been the division of Europe in regions rather than states as well as in the creation of civilizations as "the highest cultural grouping of people" [Huntington 1993, 358].

We can conclude that, first, all these factors have resulted in the erosion of nationalism in Europe as the only or the dominant mean of identification with larger groups and have opened up the way for further evolution of European identity in the form of multiple identities. The second conclusion is that, in line with Smith's [1991] and Sindic's [2008] views, national identities in Europe are strong and will not be replaced by the European identity in the foreseeable future. Though, as Eurobarometer 38 [1992, 45] reports, 23% of Europeans believed that European Identity would replace national identities. We may argue that a stronger European Identity may partially replace national identities in the future. Nevertheless, European identity is compatible with national identities and will continue to develop alongside national identities.

The EU Demos

In Chapter 3 we concluded that national identities are, to some extent, being eroded and that this erosion paved the way to the evolution of European identity as well as the emergence of a European *demos* represented by this identity. Though European identity is not fully developed and the EU is a 'sui generis' formation – hence not a state – still, as we shall demonstrate in this chapter, we can speak about the existence of a civic European *demos*, a term which does not imply the same emotional bond between its members as the nation does.

As stated in the introduction, Smith [1991, 8-9] defines two kinds of communities: cultural communities and political communities.

"Politically, there was no 'nation' in ancient Greece, only a collection of city-states, each zealous of its sovereignty. Culturally, however, there existed an ancient Greek community…A political community in turn implies at least some common institutions and a single code of rights and duties for all the members of the community. It also suggests a definite social space, a fairly well demarcated and bounded territory, with which the members identify and to which they feel they belong" [Smith 1991, 8-9].

Similar with Smith's [1991, 8] theory of 'political community', the political/legal approach argues that the civic *demos* is created through civic rights and duties, which make citizens equal and thus create a sense of solidarity in an alternative way to common culture and ethnic ties. Like constructivists, this approach argues that the EU *demos* can be engendered and constructed if there exist "common institutions and a single code of rights" [Smith, 1991, 9] and it boldly asserts that (civic) nations can be engineered.

This approach further indicates that the EU-*demos*, differently from the national *demos*, has to be conceptualized in post-national terms. Solidarity in the European political community is created by emphasizing the rights that citizens hold, which makes them co-citizens and equal to each other, which, in turn, creates a sense of community. Considering these elements of the European political community, Guler [2011, 13] argues that: "the EU-demos...has to be articulated in a different terminology than the one that has developed around the nation-state". Because of the diversity in Europe, "the EU-demos has to be articulated in terms of post-national identity" [2011, 13].

Similar with Smith's [1991, 8-9] cultural communities, the ethno/cultural approach upholds that, although there is a popular base of EU, it cannot be defined as *demos* because it is not consolidated in a social/cultural sense [Guler, 2011, 16]. Like premordialists, proponents of this theory argue that the existences of common culture as well as ethnic ties are a prerequisite for the conceptualization of *demos*. Based on the viewpoint that there is no common culture for Europe, proponents of this theory with their "No *Demos* Thesis" claim that there is no European *demos* [Brand, 2004, 7-8].

The conceptualization of the European *demos* draws from both of these community types. Although Smith [1991, 6-9] viewed these community types as mutually exclusive, both Eurosceptics and the German Federal Constitutional Court in their "No Demos Thesis" indirectly stress the necessity of the evolution of both these community types for a complete conceptualization of the European *demos*.

In this chapter we shall define *demos* from two different views. We shall demonstrate the way democracy functions in European and national levels as reported by Eurobarometer 62 [2005, 16-19] as well as will present Habermas' [2001, 15] criticism of Eurosceptics. Based on these we can maintain that there is a European civic *demos* in political/legal terms. In the second part, we will continue with the concept of the European citizenship as complementary to national citizenship as well as with scholarly conclusions about the co-existence of European and national *demos*. In the end we will argue that European and national *demo* are complementary to each other and can co-exist.

Sociology defines *demos* according to the political/legal approach. It states that *demos* is "a people which has outgrown the tribal system and is organized on the basis of neighborhood and varied modes of cooperation instead of on the basis of blood-kinship; a social body which, since blood-relationships are no longer important, includes individuals of various lineages or nationalities" [Century Dictionary Encyclopedia]. This view derives from constructivist theory which maintains that there were states which created nations. The view here is that nations are imagined and can be engendered or created [Anderson, 1991, 5-8]. Among the cases in which the states managed to create their civic nations in the absence of ethnic ties and blood-relationships we can mention US, Switzerland, and, more recently, the EU.

Weiler argues that the German Federal Constitutional Court's view that there is no *demos* without the 'Volk' (the German word for nation) was doctrinally conceived on the basis of the ethno/cultural approach on *demos*-formation and the premordialist theory which defines the nation on such ingredients like common history, language, origin and culture. Premordialists claim that nations have always existed even before states were created and, contrary to constructivists, they maintain that there were nations which created states. "The Volk pre-dates historically, and precedes politically the modern State. Germany could emerge as a modern Nation-State because there was already a German Volk" [Weiler 1995, 1].

The implication of the "No Demos Thesis" is that, as Weiler [1995, 1] maintains, in the absence of "a demos, there cannot, by definition, be a democracy or democratization at the European level". Eurobarometer 62 [2005, 16-20] reports on the way democracy works at European and national levels. It states that in

2005, 57% of the Europeans were satisfied with the way democracy worked in their own country [Eurobarometer 62, 2005, 16], while 48% were satisfied with the way democracy worked in EU level [2005, 19]. These data show that the implication derived by the No Demos Thesis – that without a European *demos* there cannot be a democracy at European level – does not appear to be valid. These data show that the level of satisfaction is nearly the same (57% vs. 48%).

Habermas [2001, 15], the theorist of 'constitutional patriotism' and the opponent of the ethno/cultural approach, as we argued in chapter 2, criticizes the "No Demos Thesis" by saying: "A nation of citizens must not be confused with a community of fate shaped by common descent, language and history. This confusion fails to capture the voluntaristic character of a civic nation, the collective identity of which exists neither independent of nor prior to the democratic process from which it springs". It is thereupon that Habermas argues about the existence of a 'civic nation'. If the willingness to be a member of the European political community, so strongly expressed in the form of the European identity, exists, why should we be based on national theories? Habermas [2001, 16] advances his thought with this question: "why, firstly, should this generation of a highly artificial kind of civic solidarity—a 'solidarity among strangers'—be doomed to come to a final halt just at the borders of our classical nation-states?". What is this generation, though? I suggest that this is precisely the generation which Smith [1991, 155] calls the new "post-industrial knowledge-based society" accentuated by globalization factors which transcend national boundaries [Chapter 3, 48].

Guler [2011, 12-20] criticizes the ethno/cultural concept of *demos*-formation based on primordial ties. This approach conceptualizes *demos* in the same way as national-*demos* have been conceptualized. Contrary to what Smith [1991, 8-9] argues, the demos in national theories "has been conceptualized both in civic as well as in ethno/cultural terms" [Guler, 2011, 19]. Guler [2011, 17] upholds that the ethno/cultural approach "has to re-conceptualize the concept of demos." Brand [2004, 13] also calls for the reconceptualization of the European *demos* in post-national terms: "We should also understand the concept of demos (and the European demos in particular)…(as) a coming together on the basis of shared values, a shared understanding of rights and societal duties and shared rational intellectual culture which transcend organic-national difference". Schmitter [2000, 28] conveys the same ideas when he asks: "Why should individuals ... in the Euro polity have to be "nationals" in some sense in order to act like citizens? Why could they not be *loyal to a common set of institutions and political/legal principles* rather than to some mystical charismatic founder or set of mythologized ancestors?" It is in these terms that Weiler considers the German Court's decision that there is no European *demos* as "a sad, (and) even pathetic decision" [Weiler, 1995].

Based on the definitions of the *demos* in political/legal terms as well as in ethno/cultural terms, on the way democracy functions in European and national levels as demonstrated by Eurobarometer 62 [2005, 16-19], as well as on the scholarly criticisms about the ethno/cultural approach and the "No Demos Thesis", we can uphold that there is a European civic *demos* defined in political/legal terms, whose existence is testified by further evidence to be presented below.

Weiler [1995, 1], only two years after the Maastricht treaty, writes that "in short, there is, want it or not, a European people on the terms stipulated by the No Demos thesis… If there is citizenship, Statehood is premised. If there is Statehood, citizenship is premised." Article 20 of the Treaty on the Functioning of the European Union states that: "Citizenship of the Union is hereby established. Every person holding the nationality of a Member State shall be a citizen of the Union. Citizenship of the Union shall be additional to and not replace national citizenship" [The Lisbon Treaty 2008, article 20]. All citizens of the E.U. member states are thus entitled to be citizens of EU.

As we argued in chapter 3, the European identity can co-exist with national identities in the form of multiple identities without conflicting or replacing them. The European citizenship, too, is additional to and does not aim to replace national citizenships. By way of inference, we can argue that the European *demos,* represented by European identity, can co-exist with national *demoi.*

In Greece and elsewhere there are European parties which compete with others in European elections. This case demonstrates the existence of the European *demos* as well as "the voluntaristic character of a civic nation" [Habermas 2001, 15]. Last but not least, it argues about the co-existence of the European *demos* with national *demos.*

Guler [2011, 21] too concludes that the European and national *demoi* can co-exist because they are different and no supersession is required for their co-existence.

> "It should be kept in mind that the EU-demos does not aim at replacing already-existing national demoi within the member states. The case of EU, therefore, directs us to re-conceptualize the demos. The EU-demos is different from the national demos. The citizens of EU do not need to be 'nationals' in the same sense as the term is used in the scale of nation-states" [2011, 21].

In sum we can uphold that there is a civic European *demos* in political/legal terms, which, like European identity, is complementary to national *demos* and co-exists without conflicting national-*demos.* The claim of Eurosceptics that the EU should not have a constitution because it does not have a *demos* does not hold true. Furthermore, it is the existence of the constitution which, through the 'constitutional patriotism', will affect in the further evolution of European identity and *demos*.

Conclusion

In 2004, at the time of the Constitutional Treaty, the European identity expressed in the form of dual identity or as a first means of identification comprised 59% of Europeans whereas national identities comprised 92% of Europeans [Eurobarometer 62,2004, 97]. Among the 59% of those who identified as Europeans, only 4% identified themselves solely as Europeans. 54% of Europeans identified with a dual identity, as Europeans and nationals simultaneously, which, as the identification with a given group also demonstrates loyalty to that group, implies a dual loyalty. The opposition camp in France, when the EU Constitutional Treaty's ratification was rejected in the ballots of the 2005 referendum, was able to manipulate this dual loyalty, expressed in the form of dual identity, and the result was a shift in the Frenchmen's loyalty from EU to their nation. There are reasons to argue that such shift of loyalty by both French and Dutch, who also rejected the constitution's ratification in a referendum, was owed to the referendum acquiring a high domestic politics character. Different political forces, as Vassallo [2007, 4] and Dinan [2010, 150] claimed, presented the European constitution as a document which was in conflict with national interest.

The EU Constitutional Treaty (2005) failed because it was immature. The European identity (with which 59% of European citizens identified themselves at the time) seemed insufficiently consolidated to influence the establishment of the constitution through 'public spheres' or direct voting. With a low degree of consolidation of European identity no approval of EU constitution, in itself marking a high degree of EU integration, could be expected. Establishing a Constitution (European constitution in our case) requires a high degree of consolidation of an identity (European identity in our case).

On the other hand, the establishment and the existence of a

65

constitution further consolidate European identity by serving as a mean in which citizens can take pride. The constitution binds its people through the Habermasian' 'constitutional patriotism' it embodies to its citizens. In other words, the Constitution and, to a lesser extent, similar institutions in the form of treaties, enhances the degree of consolidation of the European identity and of European integration.

It can be maintained that the European identity and the constitution are mutually related and affect each other. The conclusion in Chapter 2, as the Switzerland case also demonstrated, was that because of their mutual relationship, the constitution and the "civic nation" have to develop simultaneously.

Will the European identity be able to replace national identities? Many authors like Smith [1991], Sindic, Delanty, and Oner argue that European identity will not replace or supersede national identities. This is also confirmed in recent EU-Citizenship documents and actions, however, one should not neglect that globalization results in the creation of a global culture, hence, also to an erosion of nation-states [Chapter 3, 54]. International organizations such as UN and WTO and supranational entities such as the EU, too, also affect in the erosion of national identities and pave the way for the further evolution of European identity. All these factors lead to an erosion of the role of national identities as the dominant means of identification which will pave the way for further evolution of European identity in the form of multiple identities. Again we have to mention here that, as Eurobarometer 71 [2009, 36], held in the time of Lisbon Treaty, reports, the percentage of European citizens identifying themselves by way of their national identities did not decreased even after 17 years had elapsed from 1992 to 2009, but instead remained the same. This suggests that national identities are not declining. On the other hand, another reports from Eurobarometer 71 [2009, 34] demonstrates that the percentage of Europeans identifying themselves through European identity had increased from 59% in 2004 to 74% in 2009, when the

Lisbon Treaty entered into force. This suggests that European identity has developed in the form of multiple identities, which, in turn, implies that national identities are losing their role as the only or dominant means of identification, which, as we argued has occurred due to globalization factors as well as supranational organizations and human/civic rights which are no longer linked exclusively with nations. It is remarkable to note here once again that, as the Eurobarometer 38 survey indicates [1992, 45], in 1992 23% of Europeans believed that the European identity will replace the existing national identities of EU member-states. To date, though, this has not happened, but why not, perhaps a stronger European identity in the near future may partially replace national identities.

Differently from national identities, European identity develops in the fashion analyzed by post-national theory, through civic rights, "constitutional patriotism", and through its developing common culture. The European identity is *par excellence* a political identity whose solidarity is created through democratic norms and civic rights; it is founded on the recognition of human rights. Its sources of inspiration are 'constitutional patriotism' and civic rights. Its loyalty is to the constitution or constitution-like treaties. On the antipode, national identities of EU member-states are primarily based on ethnic bonds, on the perceived historical past and common culture. The solidarity they create is partial since it excludes minority groups and is based mainly on the emotional configuration attached to their membership. The loyalty of the members of the nation is to the nation itself.

Because of the difference in sources of loyalty and solidarity of European identity and national identities, we can maintain that their co-existence is possible. These two kinds of identities are different and they can co-exist in the form of multiple identities. It is the post-national nature of European identity which enables

European identity to develop alongside national identities. As Eurobarometer 38 [1992, 45] also indicates, 62% of Europeans believed that national and European identity can co-exist. Even beyond this figure, Eurobarometer 71 [2009, 34] reports that European citizens who experienced this co-existence of national and European identities, had increased from 59% in 2004 to 74% in 2009, a trend which suggests that European identity will continue to further develop in the form of multiple identities, without conflicting national identities.

Eurosceptics, in their debate with Habermas and Eurosceptics, claimed that, as there is no European *demos* (Their No Demos Thesis), the EU should not have a constitution. Criticizing them, Habermas [2001, 15] argues about the existence of European civic *demos* and nation. The conceptualization of E.U. *demos* does not require a fully developed European identity in ethno/cultural terms able to compete and replace national identities of EU member states. On the contrary, as Habermas [2001, 15] demonstrated, it requires a way of thinking different to what the ethno/cultural approach and premordial theory - in which the German Court was based in its decision of No Demos Thesis - argue about the way of *demos* formation.

By way of generalization of this book, it can be maintained that other regional organizations like the Arab League and the African Union can create collective identities similar to the EU, depending on their political unity and economic interdependence and on the existing common culture of the region able to define it as a civilization or part of it. This, however, requires specific research in the future.

Smith [1991, 153], 2 years before the Maastricht Treaty entered into force, made the same generalization. He [153] argued that the ill-fated EU model could not be spread or cloned to other continents, but, the European community with its collective identity could serve as a generalization if certain conditions which led to the emergence of the European identity are mature. Smith, however, seems to reject the post-national theory when he argues about other kinds of nationalism. "Could the European experiment become a model for other areas and associations? Clearly, the specific institutional arrangements of the new 'Europe' could not be transplanted to other continents in the manner of the ill-fated 'Westminster model'. But the European Community may well serve as a generic example if and when conditions elsewhere are ripe; and, as I shall argue, that ripeness may well depend, paradoxically, on the progress of certain cultural conditions, notably certain kinds of nationalism" [1991, 153].

BIBLIOGRAPHY

Primary sources & documents

Commission of the European Communities (Dec, 1992), *Eurobarometer 38. Public opinion in the European Community,* Brusesels; available online and retrieved on June 15, 2012 from:

> http://ec.europa.eu/public_opinion/archives/eb/eb38/eb38_en.htm

--------(Nov, 1998), *Eurobarometer 50. Public opinion in the European Community,* Brusesels; available online and retrieved on June 15, 2012 from: http://europa.eu.int/en/comm/dg10/infcom/epo/eb.html

--------(October 2000), *Eurobarometer 53. Public opinion in the European Community,* Brussels;

> available online and retrieved on June 31, 2012 from: http://ec.europa.eu/public_opinion/archives/eb/eb53/eb53_en.htm

--------(Dec. 2000), *Eurobarometer 54. Public opinion in the European Community,* Brusesels; available online and retrieved on June 15, 2012 from: http://ec.europa.eu/public_opinion/archives/eb/eb54/eb54_en.htm

--------(Oct. 2001), *Eurobarometer 56. Public opinion in the European Community,* Brusesels; available online and retrieved on June 15, 2012 from: http://ec.europa.eu/public_opinion/archives/eb/eb56/eb56_en.htm

--------(Nov. 2002), *Eurobarometer 58. Public opinion in the European Community,* Brusesels; available online and retrieved on June 15, 2012 from: http://ec.europa.eu/public_opinion/archives/eb/eb58/eb58_en.htm

--------(Nov. 2003), *Eurobarometer 60. Public opinion in the European Community,* Brusesels; available online and retrieved on June 15, 2012 from: http://ec.europa.eu/public_opinion/archives/eb/eb60/eb60_en.htm

--------(Nov. 2004), *Eurobarometer 62. Public opinion in the European Community,* Brusesels; available online and retrieved on June 15, 2012 from: http://ec.europa.eu/public_opinion/archives/eb/eb62/eb62_en.htm

--------(Nov. 2005), *Eurobarometer 64. Public opinion in the European Community,* Brusesels; available online and retrieved on June 15, 2012 from: http://ec.europa.eu/public_opinion/archives/eb/eb64/eb64_en.htm

--------(June 2009), *Eurobarometer 71. Public opinion in the European Community,* Brusesels; available online and retrieved on June 15, 2012 from: http://ec.europa.eu/public_opinion/archives/eb/eb71/eb71_en.htm

Business Dictionary. Globalization. Retrieved on November, 30, 2011, from http://www.businessdictionary.com/definition/globalization.html

Council of Europe. The founding Fathers. Retrieved on 5, July 2012

from:
http://www.coe.int/aboutcoe/index.asp?page=peresFondateurs

CVCE (2001). LAEKEN DECLARATION ON THE FUTURE OF THE EUROPEAN UNION. Retrieved on March 26, 2012, from: http://european-convention.eu.int/pdf/lknen.pdf

Euroacademia (2012). How cosmopolitan is European identity. Retrieved on May 5, 2012, from: http://euroacademia.eu/presentation/how-cosmopolitan-is-european-identity/

European Commission [I] (2012). Justice. EU Citizenship. Retrieved on July, 27, 2012, from: http://ec.europa.eu/justice/citizen/

European Commission [II] (2012) *Small and medium sized enterprise (SMs).* Retrieved on July 10, 2012, from: http://ec.europa.eu/enterprise/policies/sme/facts-figures-analysis/sme-observatory/index_en.htm

European Commission [III] (2012). Regional Pilocy- Inforegio. Retrived on July 15, 2012, from: http://ec.europa.eu/regional_policy/thefunds/ipa/strategic_en.cfm

European Union (2007). "The emerging European identity". Retrieved on March 20, 2012, from: http://www.eurunion.org/news/eunewsletters/EUFocus/2007/EUFocus-Identity2007.pdf

European Union (2011). Europa; EU symbols. Retrieved on November, 19, 2011, from http://www.google.com/#sclient=psy- -

European Union. The history of the European Union. Robert Schuman (1886-1963). Retrieved on August 10, 2012, from: http://europa.eu/about-eu/eu-history/1945-

1959/foundingfathers/schuman/index_en.htm

INTERREG IVC. About the programme. Retrieved on July 9, 2012, from: http://i4c.eu/about_programme.html

Socrates Programme. First Step. European Community action programme in the field of education (2000-2006). Retrieved on July 10, 2012, from: http://www.firststeps-project.eu/web/content.asp?lng=en&section=SOCRATES

Switzerland (2010). The federal Constitution of the Swiss Confederation, September 12 1848. Kessinger Publishing, 2010. Available on: http://books.google.com/books?id=xcUGAAAAYAAJ&prints ec=frontcover&source=gbs_ge_summary_r&cad=0#v=onepag e&q&f=true

Switzerland's History. History of Switzerland. Switzerland's Way towards the Federal Constitution of 1848. Retrieved on July, 20, from: http://history-switzerland.geschichte-schweiz.ch/switzerland-federal-constitution-1848.html

The Lisbon Treaty. Retrieved on July, 24, from: http://www.lisbon-treaty.org/wcm/the-lisbon-treaty.html

The Maastricht Treaty (1992). Provisions amending the treaty Establishing the European economic Community with a view to establishing the European community. Retrieved on July 10, 2012, from: http://www.eurotreaties.com/maastrichtec.pdf

Scholarly Reflections

Anderson, B. (1991). *Imagined Communities*. Revised Edition. Verso. London: New York.

Balibar, E. Wallerstain, I, (1991). *Local Histories/Global Designs*. Chichester: Princenton University.

Bakke, E. (1993). Toward a European Identity? Arena Working Paper No. 10/1995.

Beta (2012). This house believes Europe still needs a constitution. Idebate. Org. 22 Feb 2012. Idebate.org, Web. 31 Aug 2012.

Bismarck, J. (2008). "Why Pigs Can't fly". *Newsweek Magazine.* Retrieved on July 5, 2012, from: http://www.thedailybeast.com/newsweek/2008/06/28/why-pigs-can-t-fly.html

Brand, M. (2004). *Affirming and Refining European Constitutionalism: Towards the Establishment of the First Constitution for the European Union.* European University Institute: Italy.

Breda, V. (2011). Constitutional patriotism: A Reasonable Theory of Radical Democracy? (August 26, 2011).

Cinpoes, R. (2008). THEMATIC ARTICLES – NATIONAL IDENTITY AND EUROPEAN IDENTITY. From National Identity to European Identity. *Journal of* Identity *and Migration Studies. Volume 2, Number 1, 2008.*

Conversi, D. (2006) *Mapping the field: theories of nationalism and the ethnosymbolic approach.* In: Leoussi, Athena S. and Grosby, Steven, (eds.) *(2006).* Nationalism and ethnosymbolism: history, culture and ethnicity in the formation of nations. Edinburgh: Edinburgh University Press.

Cottey, A. (2007). *Security.* Palgrave Mackmillan. New York.

Delanly (2005). What does it mean to be a 'European'? *Innovation, Vol. 18, No. 1, 2005.*

Delantly, G. (1996). Beyond the Nation-State: national Identity and Citizenship in a Multicultural Society- A Response to Rex. *Sociological Research Online,* vol. 1, no. 3,

Delanty, G. (2003). Is there a European Identity? *GLOBAL DIALOGUE Volume 5 Number 3–4 Summer/Autumn 2003.*

Delanty, G. (2009). *The Cosmopolitan Imagination: The Renewal of Critical Social Theory.* Cambridge University Press. UK.

Dinan, D. (2010). Ever Closer Union. 4th Edition. Palgrave: Mackmillan

Druckman, D. (2010). Nationalism, Patriotism, and Group Loyalty: A Social Psychological Perspective. Mershon International Studies Review, Vol. 38, No. 1 (Apr., 1994), pp. 43-68.

Eriksen, E. (2009) *Unfinished Democratization of Europe.* Oxford: Oxford University Press. ISBN-13: 9780199572519.

Edwards, M. (2009). *Civil Society.* Great Britain: MPG Books LTD. ISBN: 13-978-0-7456-4584-8.

European Comission. Enlargement. Planning of the IPA. Retrieved on July 10, 2012, from: http://ec.europa.eu/enlargement/how-does-it-work/financial-assistance/planning-ipa_en.htm

European Navigator (Sept. 2010). Early history of the European integration after WW II. Retrievd on July 5, 2012, from: http://cclleu.eu/cms02/fileadmin/daten/Dateien/teaching_material/Deutschland/History_of_European_integration.pdf

Gregston, B. (2005). France turns against Europe. *Worldpress.org contributing editor Paris, France.*

Guler, Z. (2011). Demos Formation in the European Union and Turkish Accession in the EU– Does the Definition of EU-Demos IncludeTurkey?. Master Thesis. Upssala University Press.

Habermas, J. (2001). Why Europe needs a constitution. *New Left Review*, v. 11 (Sept.-Oct. 2001).

Hayes, C. (2016). *Nationalism: A religion.* Routledge

Herman, M. (2004). *Advances in Political Psychology.* Vol. 1. Elsevier Ltd 84 Theobalds Road London WCIX8RR UK. ISBN: 0-08-043989-6.

Hobson, B. (2003) *'Recognition Struggles and Social Movements.* UK: Combridge University Press.

Hojlund, N. (2009). What is European Identity? Retrieved on February 26, 2012, from: http://www.ffd.dk/media/11298/eu_niels.pdf

Huntington, S. (1993). The Clash of Civilizations. *Foreign Affairs,* Vol. 72. No. 3. Pp. 22-49.

Jackobs, D. Maire, J. (1998). European identity: construct, fact and fiction. In Gastelaars, M. – Ruijter, A. (eds.) (1998). *A United Europe. The Quest for a Multifaceted Identity.* Maastricht: Shaker, pp. 13-34.

Kaelberer, M. (2004). The Euro and European Identity: Symbols, Power and the Politics of European Monetary Union. *Review of International Studies Vol. 30, April 2004, 161-178*

Kral, D. (2006). The Constitution is dead. Long live the Treaty of Nice? Retrieved on May 16, 2012, from: http://www.europeum.org/doc/pdf/836.pdf

Leoussi, A. Smith, A. (2001). *Encyclopedia of Nationalism.* Transaction Publishers, Rutgers: New Jersey. USA. ISBN 0-7658-0002-0.

Maastricht Treaty. (2012). In *Encyclopædia Britannica.* Retrieved on May 15, from: http://www.britannica.com/EBchecked/topic/196490/Maastricht-Treaty

Monnet, J. Schuman, R. (2005). European Identity and the Challenge of Enlargement. *Jean Monnet/Robert Schuman Paper Series. Vol.5 No. 31*

Muller, J (2007) *Constitutional Patriotism.* Princeton. Edu. USA. ISBN 978-0-691-11859-8.

Oner, S. (2004). The Limits of European Integration: The Question of European Identity. *Ankara Avrupa Çalismaları Dergisi*, v. 3/2, pp. 27-38.

Petithome, M. (2008). Is there a European Identity? National Attitudes and Social Identification toward the European Union. *Journal of Identity and Migration Studies*, v. 2/1, pp. 15-36

Prisacariu, S. (2007). The Symbols role in the creation of a European Identity. Master's Thesis. University of IASI.

Rambour, M. (2005).References and uses of Post-nationalism in French and British debates on Europe. Presented in Workshop.

Reilly, K. (2004). *Worlds of History.* Second edition. Bendford: St. Martin's.

Rex, J. (1996). 'National identity in the Democratic Mutli-Cultural State' *Sociological research Online,* vol. 1, no. 2.

Risse, Th. Grabowsky, J. (2008). European Identity Formation in the Public Spheres and in Foreign Policy. RECON online working paper 2008/04. ISSN 1504-6907.

Rousseau, D. Veen, M. (2005). The Emergence of a Shared Identity. *.Journal of Conflic Conflict Resolution*, v. 49/5, pp. 686-712.

Schuman, R. (1950). Schuman Declaration and the Birth of Europe. Speech of 9 May 1950.

Sindic, D. (2008). National identities: are they declining?. *Beyond Current Horizons.* Retrieved on   November 28, 2011, from http://www.beyondcurrenthorizons.org.uk/national-identities-are-they-declining/

Smith, A. (1991). *National Identity*. London: Penguin Books.

Stojanovic, N (2003). Swiss nation-state and its patriotism A critique of Will Kymlicka's account of multination states. *Polis / R.C.S.P./C.P.S.R. Vol. 11, Numéros Spécial 2003.*

Swissuniversity. History of Switzerland. Four official languages: The Roman heritage and the German migration. Retrieved on September 10, 2012, from: http://www.swissuniversity.ch/country-history.htm

Tajfel, H. (1981). *Human Groups and Social categories.* Cambridge University Press, USA. ISBN 0 521 22839 5.

The Lisbon Treaty. (2008). *The Lisbon Treaty*. Third Edition. Foundation for EU Democracy: Denmark. ISBN: 87-87692-72-4.

Thomas, D. Schult, Ch. Zuber, H. (2011). Citizens of the EU. How to Forge a Common European Identity. *DER SPEIGEL 48/2011 (Nov. 28, 2011).*

Uwosomah, A. (2010). European Identity over national identity. Unpublished Master Thesis.

Valentini, Ch. (2005). The promotion of European identity. retrieved on May 5, 2012, from: http://www.chiara-valentini.org/the_promotion_of_european_identity_book%20version.pdf

Vassallo, F. (2007). The failed EU Constitution referendums: The French case in perspective, 1992 and 2005. *Prepared for the first Annul research Conference of the EU Center of Excellence (EUCE)at Dalhausie University, Halifax, Canada, May 21-23, 2007.*

Wailer, J. (1995). Demos, Telos and the German Maastricht Decision. Retrieved on July, 25, 2012, from :

http://centers.law.nyu.edu/jeanmonnet/archive/papers/95/9506ind.html

Walkenhorst, H. *The conceptual spectrum of European identity-From Missing Link to Unecesary Evil.* University of Limerick: Ireland. ISBN: 1-905952-18-X.

White, T. (2010). European integration, identity, and national self interest: the enduring nature of national identity. Unpublished PhD Dissertation.

Made in the USA
Middletown, DE
25 March 2018